STUDY IN CANADA

A step-by-step guide for international students

Author: Raghid Shreih

Publication Date: November 1, 2023

ISBN: 978-1-7779500-3-3

Copyright © 2023 Ya Hala Canada Immigration Inc. All rights reserved.

Study in Canada
A step-by-step guide for international students

Important Notice!

The information provided in this book is for general information and educational purposes only. It is not to be understood as legal advice or immigration consultation advice. If you want an immigration consultation, please contact Ya Hala Canada Immigration Inc. to discuss.

Copyright © 2023 Ya Hala Canada Immigration Inc. All rights reserved.

All rights reserved. No part of this book may be reproduced in any form or by any electronic or mechanical means, including information storage and retrieval systems, without written permission from the author, except in the case of a reviewer, who may quote brief passages embodied in critical articles or in a review.

40% of all Canada study permit applications are refused!

After getting admitted into a Canadian educational institution, many international students think that getting a Canadian study permit is automatic, and that it is just a formality. Statistics published by the Department of Immigration, Refugees and Citizenship Canada (IRCC) indicates that the overall study permit approval rate is only 60%[1]! This means that the other 40%, which is nearly half of all applications, is refused!

Why do study permit applications get refused? What are Canadian immigration officers looking for in an application? How can you ensure that you present your application in a way that maximizes your chance of being approved?

This book covers these questions, and much more. It will take you on a journey from learning about Canada, the advantages of studying in Canada, getting admission to a Canadian educational institution, getting your study permit, and finally traveling to and arriving in Canada!

_____

[1] **Source:** Data represents the approval rate between January 1, 2019 and December 31, 2021, as published by "CIMM – Student Approval Rates by Country of Residence – February 15 and 17, 2022".

It then goes further to discuss some tips about studying in Canada, what to expect, and your options after graduation, including staying in Canada, getting a work permit, applying for permanent residency, or returning to your home country.

A dedicated section discusses study permit refusals, what to do if you receive a refusal, and strategies to maximize your chance of getting an approval!

Dedication

To all the honest, principled, hard working people across the globe looking for freedom, economic opportunity, and the protection of their rights.

To all those who look to Canada, let's make this country an example of a free, prosperous, virtuous, and proud nation where diversity, equity, and lending a helping hand makes us stronger and better, together!

And to Canada and all of its people, a nation that accepted my family when we were stateless and weak. A nation that welcomed us as citizens and equals. A nation that gave us our rights and freedoms for the first time in our lives. A nation that in return has earned our never wavering love and loyalty for generations to come. Let us never change!

> With glowing hearts we see thee rise,
> The True North strong and free!
> From far and wide,
> O Canada, we stand on guard for thee.
> God keep our land glorious and free!

Table Of Contents

Introduction...13
About Ya Hala Canada Immigration Inc................................. 16
The 7 Steps to Studying in Canada.......................................21

STEP 1: Choosing Canada

Why Should You Consider Studying in Canada?.................... 25
    Canadian Geography and Climate....................................... 28
    Overview of Canadian History and Government.................32
    The Canadian Economy... 36
    The Charter of Rights and Freedoms...................................37
    Canada's Post-Secondary Education System..................... 39
    International Students in Canada..45
    Advantages of Studying in Canada..................................... 48
        Quality of Education.. 48
        Diversity and Multiculturalism..................................... 49
        Safety..49
        Cost of Living and Tuition Fees..................................... 50
        Working During Studies and After Graduation.............51
        Keeping the Family Together..52
        Pathway to Permanent Residency................................53

STEP 2: Getting Admission

Getting Admission to an Educational Institution in Canada.................. 61
    Finding the Right Institution And Program..........................61
    Applications and Admissions...68

STEP 3: Getting a Study Permit

Getting a Study Permit..77
- Overview of the process..79
- Student Direct Stream (SDS)...82
- General Requirements..84
- Key Considerations..90
- Tips & Tricks..92
- Bringing your Family..108
  - Spousal Open Work Permits..109
  - Visitor Visas...111
  - Minor Children and Schooling..112
  - Maintaining a Valid Status..113
- Hire a professional...113
- Approvals and Refusals..114
- Get To Know Your Study Permit...115
  - Visa vs. eTA...115
  - When/Where is a study permit issued?....................................116
  - What information is on the study permit?.................................118
  - Key Dates on the Study Permit..119
  - Study Permit Conditions..120

Study Permit Refusals..121
- Study Permit Refusal Rates..122
- What to do if your Study Permit Application is Refused?..............126
- GCMS Notes..129
- Re-Application Strategy...133
- Organizing your subsequent application......................................135

STEP 4: Arriving in Canada

Travel and Arrival in Canada **143**
    What to Bring with you to Canada? 146
    Accommodations 148

STEP 5: Studying in Canada

Studying in Canada **157**
    Key skills to develop 157
    Course planning 159
    Academic expectations 161
    Cheating and Plagiarism 163
    Working While You Study 165

STEP 6: After You Graduate

After you Graduate **171**
    Study Permit Expiry 172
    Returning to your home country 173
    Extending your Stay in Canada 176
        Stay in Canada for Further Studies 176
        Stay in Canada as a Visitor 178
        Stay in Canada as a Worker 179
    Post-Graduate Work Permit (PGWP) 180

The Path to Permanent Residency **187**

STEP 7: Hire Professional Help

Get Professional Help with your Visa and Immigration Needs **197**
    But Internet Discussion Boards are Full of Immigration Advice! 198
    Applying Independently Without Professional Help 199
    Immigration Fraud and Unlicensed Immigration Consultants 200
    Ya Hala Canada Immigration Inc. 202

Conclusion..	**206**
Important Legal Notice..	**209**
Appendix A: Study Permit Approval Rates By Country.......	**215**
Appendix B: CRS Points Grid...	**221**

Introduction

Canada has been a top destination for international students for many decades. While some studies report that the first international students came to study in Canada as early as the 1800s, the number of students coming to Canada has increased rapidly since the middle of the twentieth century. Students choose Canada as a top destination to pursue their studies for many reasons, such as safety, diversity, high quality of education, lower costs of living compared to other developed countries, and the possibility of permanent residency and settlement in Canada.

In this book, we will discuss why students choose Canada and share statistics about where these students come from and which provinces they study in. We will also cover many reasons that make Canada one of the best places to pursue studies. Although studying in Canada is open to minor students under some circumstances, this book will focus on students interested in post-secondary education at the college or university level. To keep the terminology simple, we will often refer to all types of post-secondary educational institutions as universities.

The book also gives an overview of the journey to becoming a student in Canada, from the early steps of selecting a school and a program all the way to arriving in Canada. The study permit application process is

discussed to understand the requirements and procedures for applying for a study permit. Study permit refusals are also discussed, as well as options and strategies for dealing with them. Advice for students on academic expectations is also provided, along with information about working during and after the study program.

Finally, post-study options are discussed, including returning to your home country and exploring options for immigration and permanent residency in Canada.

We are honored at Ya Hala Canada Immigration Inc. to support foreign students in their journey to study in Canada, work after graduation, and apply for permanent residency if they want to settle in Canada. We have hundreds of students with their study permit applications, and we would be happy to support you as well. Please visit our website or contact us to discuss your specific circumstances and requirements.

Please note that the information provided in this book is intended to be purely for informational and educational purposes and is not to be understood as legal or immigration consulting advice. The book is intended to provide you with general information on what to expect. However, each person's situation is different, and so the information provided in the book may not apply to you. Also, immigration rules and

regulations change frequently, and so the information in this book may not be up-to-date.

It is highly recommended to work with a lawyer or a Regulated Canadian Immigration Consultant (RCIC) for all your immigration applications.

About Ya Hala Canada Immigration Inc.

Our company, Ya Hala Canada Immigration Inc., provides Canadian immigration consulting services through our Regulated Canadian Immigration Consultant (RCIC) Raghid Shreih (registration #: R528761). This includes not only study permits, but also work permits, visitor visas, permanent residency, and family sponsorships.

We published this book as a resource to all those interested in immigration to Canada, whether temporarily to study or work, or permanently to settle and live in Canada and eventually obtain Canadian citizenship. This resource was specifically designed for those interested in pursuing post-secondary studies at a Canadian college or university.

At Ya Hala Canada Immigration Inc., we believe in carefully listening to the needs of our clients and tailoring our services to what they need. Every client is unique and has special circumstances, and we do our best to provide services that fit each client's needs.

With our full representation services, we help our clients through the entire application process, from the initial consultation, through getting to know our clients and their particular situation, advising them on the best strategy to accomplish their goals regarding immigration to Canada, complete the entire application process, including paperwork and

gathering and submitting required documents, and following up on their application until a final decision is made by the Government of Canada. We can also customize a package of services to meet each client's specific needs and budget.

Alternatively, we also offer hourly consultations that can be extremely helpful to get a Regulated Canadian Immigration Consultant (RCIC) to answer your questions about immigration to Canada, discuss a specific issue you are facing, or review your documents and forms prior to submission.

We are registered with the CICC (College of Immigration and Citizenship Consultants), the national regulatory body that oversees regulated Canadian immigration professionals. So when you work with Ya Hala Canada Immigration, you can be confident that you are working with legitimate and responsible Canadian immigration professionals.

Our team has over 20 years of experience helping hundreds of clients immigrate and settle in Canada. We provide comprehensive services, including Canadian Permanent Residence (PR) and temporary residence applications. Our goal is not to simply process your application but to help you at every step of the way to minimize your stress and worry and to get you settled and started on the path to success in Canada!

 **Ya Hala Canada Immigration
Professional. Trusted. Secure.**

Services We Provide	
Canadian Permanent Residence (PR) Applications	Express Entry, Federal Skilled Workers (FSWP), Federal Skilled Trades (FSTP), Canadian Experience Class (CEC), Business immigrants, Entrepreneurs and Investors, Self-Employed, Start-up Visa, Provincial Nomination Programs (PNPs), and Family Sponsorship.
Temporary Residence Applications	Study permits, Post-Graduate Work Permits (PGWP), Work permits, Visitor Visa, Parents and Grandparents Super Visa

	Why Choose Ya Hala Canada Immigration Inc.
Experience:	Our staff has over 20 years of experience helping clients with immigration and settlement services. We have seen many scenarios over the years, and we know how to handle any situation.
Integrity:	Honesty and integrity are our most important values. We will work hard on your behalf because we know the impact of our work on the lives of our clients and their families. We want to see you succeed and achieve all your goals in Canada.
Regulated Professionals:	When you work with an RCIC, you know that an expert is advising you on Canadian immigration who is professional and is regulated by the CICC (College of Immigration and Citizenship Consultants). Beware of unlicensed and unregulated consultants. If they cannot abide by the rules in their own profession, how can you trust them to make sure your immigration applications adhere to all the rules and regulations to ensure a successful result?
Tailored Services:	Whether you are looking for full representation, just need some help through the process, or would like an hourly consultation, we are ready to help!

The 7 Steps to Studying in Canada

STEP 1: Choosing Canada

STEP 2: Getting Admission

STEP 3: Getting a Study Permit

STEP 4: Arriving in Canada

STEP 5: Studying in Canada

STEP 6: After You Graduate

STEP 7: Hire Professional Help

STEP 1: Choosing Canada

Why Should You Consider Studying in Canada?

There are a number of destinations that are popular for international students. Besides Canada, students often choose countries like the USA, UK, or Australia to pursue their post-secondary studies. So what makes Canada special? Is Canada the right country for you to choose for your college or university education?

International students have to consider many factors when choosing where they want to complete their post-secondary education. Studying abroad is a big investment and a major life decision. International students will often be away from their families and friends for a long period of time during their studies. They will lose their support networks, and will have to face the uncertainty of living in a new country and a new culture. This can be scary and cause a lot of worry, especially for students who have had limited or no previous travel experience. A lot of planning and consideration should go into making such a big decision.

A major consideration for students is the financial cost of studying abroad. Going to a college or university in another country is quite expensive. In addition to the costs of tuition fees, students must also cover their living costs including rent, food, transportation, telephone and internet bills, and other miscellaneous costs.

Another major consideration is the quality of education offered by educational institutions in the country that you choose. Many of the top universities globally are in North America, Europe, and Australia. Students should carefully consider the reputation of the institutions they consider and the quality of the education that they will receive. Making a major investment in your education can be a very wise decision if the return on your investment will be very high. In many cases, gaining a degree from a top college or university unlocks great work opportunities and higher compensation that can quickly pay back the money invested in your education.

Students must also consider the culture of the country that they are planning to study. Is the country known to welcome international students? Are there many cultures represented in the college or university environment that they will be living in? Will you be able to feel safe, make friends, and practice your religion and culture freely? Students appreciate the opportunity to study in a diverse and multicultural educational institution where they will interact with people from around the world.

Many students are interested in gaining international work experience post-graduation. So it is important to consider whether the country that you are planning to study in offers opportunities to work during and after

graduation. Working during or after graduation can be a great way to recover the costs of your education. It can also provide you with valuable international work experience that will help you to find better and higher paying job opportunities when you return to your home country. It is also important to consider whether there is a pathway to permanent residency or longer term work permits in case you decide to stay for some time after graduation.

This chapter will give an overview about Canada and provide you with enough information to make an educated decision about whether studying in Canada is the best choice for you.

Summary: Factors to Consider When Choosing a University

Make a table listing all the universities you are considering, and score each one from 1 to 10 for each of the following factors. Then add up the numbers to see which university scores the highest.

- Quality of Education
- Total cost (tuition fees + living expenses)
- Supportive and diverse culture
- Ability to work while you study
- Post-graduation work opportunities
- Pathways to permanent residency
- Return-on-investment (post-graduation salary vs. total cost)

Canadian Geography and Climate

Canada is in the North American continent and is the second-largest country in the world by land area. It shares land borders with only one country, the United States of America. The Canada-USA border is the longest international border between any two countries in the world. Canada is bounded by three oceans: the Atlantic Ocean in the east, the Pacific Ocean in the west, and the Arctic Ocean in the north. Only two Canadian provinces are landlocked: Alberta and Saskatchewan. The remaining provinces and territories all have access to one of the three oceans surrounding Canada.

The following map illustrates the 10 provinces and 3 territories that make up Canada.

Figure 1: Map of Canadian Provinces and Territories [2]

---

[2] **Source:** Map courtesy of E Pluribus Anthony
http://commons.wikimedia.org/wiki/File:Political_map_of_Canada.png

Copyright © 2023 - Ya Hala Canada Immigration Inc. - All rights reserved

\multicolumn{3}{c}{Canada's Provinces and Territories}		
Abbreviation	Province	Major Cities
AB	Alberta	Edmonton, Calgary
BC	British Columbia	Vancouver, Victoria, Kelowna, Abbotsford
MB	Manitoba	Winnipeg, Brandon
NB	New Brunswick	Moncton, Fredericton, Saint John
NL	Newfoundland and Labrador	St. John's, Corner Brook
NS	Nova Scotia	Halifax, Sydney
ON	Ontario	Toronto, Ottawa, Hamilton, Kitchener-Waterloo, London, Windsor, Kingston
PE	Prince Edward Island (PEI)	Charlottetown, Summerside
QC	Quebec	Montreal, Quebec City, Gatineau, Sherbrooke, Trois-Rivières
SK	Saskatchewan	Saskatoon, Regina
Abbreviation	Territory	Major Cities
NT	Northwest Territories	Yellowknife
YT	Yukon	Whitehorse
NU	Nunavut	Iqaluit

Copyright © 2023 - Ya Hala Canada Immigration Inc. - All rights reserved

Canada has over two million lakes, including shared access to four of the five Great Lakes, giving it the world's largest proportion of freshwater. The province of Ontario shares access to Lake Ontario, Lake Erie, Lake Huron, and Lake Superior with the United States.

Canada's climate varies between provinces and territories. The extreme north of Canada has a snowy polar climate most of the year. However, most of Canada experiences four distinct seasons. Many people are surprised to know that Canada can experience heat waves in the summer season, where temperatures can approach 40° degrees Celsius (100°+ degrees Fahrenheit). Winters can be bitterly cold, with temperatures remaining below freezing for substantial periods during winter. Cold spells can bring temperatures down to -40° degrees Celsius (-40° degrees Fahrenheit) across large parts of Canada. The exception to this is the province of British Columbia which experiences significantly milder winters than the rest of Canada due to the moderating impact of the Pacific Ocean.

Canada's population reached 40 million people in 2023, about half of whom live in the approximately 1,150 kilometer corridor running from Windsor in southwestern Ontario to Quebec City to the northeast. The Quebec City – Windsor Corridor is Canada's most densely populated region and includes the Greater Toronto Area (GTA), Montreal,

Ottawa-Gatineau, and Quebec City. Outside of this corridor, major Canadian cities include Vancouver in British Columbia, Calgary and Edmonton in Alberta, and Winnipeg in Manitoba.

Overview of Canadian History and Government

Centuries before Europeans arrived in North America and established settlements there, Canada was populated by First Nations and Inuit societies, including the Huron, Iroquois, Cree, Dene, Sioux, and Inuit. Some of these societies depended on hunting and migrating across the land, searching for food and resources. Others farmed and had established communities with complex governmental systems, including village and tribal councils that made major decisions by consensus.

Although there is evidence that Vikings established some settlements in Canada as early as the year 1000, it was not until the end of the fifteenth century (around the year 1500) that the first European settlers began to arrive, including Italian, Spanish, Portuguese, French and British pioneers. Control of Canada eventually rested with the British, and Canada remained under British control after the American revolution.

On July 1, 1867, the Dominion of Canada was formed and Canada emerged as a self-governing colony of the British Empire. It consisted of only four provinces: Ontario, Quebec, Nova Scotia and New Brunswick.

Canada continued to grow with new provinces joining the confederation, with the last province to join being Newfoundland in 1949. We continue to celebrate July 1st of each year as "Canada Day", as it is the day when Canada was first formed as a nation.

Canada is a Constitutional Monarchy, as it is part of the Commonwealth whose monarch as of 2023 is Charles III. The monarch appoints a representative, the governor-general, to carry out royal duties in Canada. However, the actual government in Canada is based on a parliamentary system. Each of the 338 members of parliament in the House of Commons is elected within their electoral district. The party with the largest number of seats in parliament forms the government and its head becomes the Prime Minister of Canada. Provinces have a similar system for electing provincial representatives, with the head of the winning party becoming the premier of the province.

As a Confederation, government powers in Canada are divided between the Federal government and the Provincial and Territorial governments. For example, the provincial governments are responsible for health, education, most social programs, civil and property rights, and power over local government. The federal government is responsible for international trade, communications, transportation, banking, currency, foreign affairs, defense, and immigration, among others.

Canadian cities also have municipal governments, formed by city councillors elected by residents of each electoral district or riding. Residents also vote for a mayor who is the head of the municipal government. These local governments are responsible for local issues such as local police, roadways, parking, libraries, parks, and community water systems.

Canadian citizens have a strong say in their government and are responsible for electing representatives at the federal level to parliament in Ottawa, provincial representatives to their provincial parliament, and mayors and councillors to represent them at the municipal level. Residents are also often responsible for voting for members of their local school boards.

Figure 2: The Château Frontenac, Quebec city [3]

---

[3] **Source:** Wilfredor, CC0, via Wikimedia Commons
https://commons.wikimedia.org/wiki/File:Ch%C3%A2teau_Frontenac,_Quebec_city,_Canada.jpg

The Canadian Economy

Canada is a developed country with a market economy and is among the largest economies in the world by GDP. Canada is rich in natural resources, and is a major producer and exporter of oil and gas, potash, uranium, gold, diamonds, iron ore, and softwood lumber. In addition to Canada's significant natural resource sector, Canada has highly developed service and manufacturing sectors. Canadian manufacturing includes automobiles, aviation, high tech, steel, among others. Canada also has a large agricultural sector and is a major exporter of agricultural products to the United States and Asia. In 2018, Canadian exports reached close to 600 million Canadian dollars.

Although Canada's largest trading partner is the United States due to the close proximity and long border between the two nations, Canada also has trade relationships with many other countries. This includes free trade agreements with the United States and Mexico, Europe, Japan, Chile, and Australia.

Canada's oil and gas industry is centered around the province of Alberta, where most of the petroleum resources are located. Canada is the fourth-largest producer and exporter of oil globally, and 96% of Canada's

oil exports go to the United States. Canada has about 10% of the world's proven oil reserves, mostly in the form of oil sands.

Manufacturing represents over 10% of Canada's GDP, or approximately 174 billion Canadian dollars. Manufacturers export more than 350 billion Canadian dollars each year, which is over 60% of Canada's total exports. This strong manufacturing sector provides nearly 1.7 million full-time jobs for engineers, technicians, researchers, designers, programmers and tradespeople.

Canada's economy is constantly in search of new skilled workers, which explains the immigration policies of Canada that encourage the immigration of skilled workers and the strategy of accepting large numbers of international students each year. International students who study in Canada are an important source of skilled workers for Canada's economy.

The Charter of Rights and Freedoms

One of the great attractions that makes thousands of immigrants want to settle in Canada each year is the freedom and rights that Canadian citizens enjoy. In 1982, the Canadian Charter of Rights and Freedoms became part of Canada's Constitution. The Charter enshrines the rights of all Canadians to be treated equally under the law. It guarantees

Canadians fundamental rights such as freedom of expression, freedom of the press, freedom of assembly, and freedom of religion.

The Charter also protects Canadians' democratic rights, including the right to vote and serve as an elected representative in government. It also protects the right of movement into and out of Canada, and movement between Canada's provinces and territories. It protects Canadians' right to life, liberty, and security, freedom from unreasonable search and arbitrary detention, the right to legal counsel, the right to be presumed innocent until proven guilty, and many other key legal rights.

Crucially, the Charter enshrines multiculturalism as a core Canadian value by emphasizing the preservation and enhancement of the multicultural heritage of Canadians. This has transformed Canadian society into a rich mixture of cultures from around the world, with no single culture or religion having an official preference over others.

Multiculturalism has made Canada an attractive destination for immigrants and international students because it welcomes the diversity of cultures and languages from around the world. Canadian communities from different backgrounds often establish local community groups and centers and continue to practice and hold onto their cultural heritage, language, and religion while integrating into overall Canadian society.

Canada's Post-Secondary Education System

Since this book is directed towards those pursuing post-secondary studies in Canada, we will focus on Canada's post-secondary education system. Prospective students need to have some appreciation of how the education system works to be able to understand the various study programs and institutions that are available.

Canadian children typically start attending formal school at the age of 6. Primary schooling starts at grade 1, and students progress to grade 12, which is the final year of secondary school (also known as high school). Post-Secondary education refers to study programs beyond secondary school. Therefore, a prerequisite to studying at Canadian post-secondary institutions will almost always be a high school diploma.

The province of Quebec has a slightly different system. Primary schooling still consists of grades 1 - 6, but secondary school only goes until grade 11. Beyond grade 11, students interested in pursuing higher education enroll in colleges known as CEGEP, which is an acronym from the French term Collège d'enseignement général et professionnel (which translates to English as General and professional teaching college). These colleges act as a preparation stage for students to determine whether they want to continue on to university, or to study a vocational skill that allows them

to enter the job market directly. Students intending to go on to university generally spend two years studying at a CEGEP, while those studying technical skills typically require three years of full-time study.

Post-secondary educational institutions in Canada fall into one of two types: universities and colleges. Universities offer bachelor's, master's, and doctoral degrees, and other post-graduate certificates and diplomas. Some universities are focused only on undergraduate programs at the bachelor's level, while others also offer graduate research programs that award master's and doctoral degrees.

On the other hand, colleges typically offer diplomas and certificates that don't rise to a full bachelor's degree level. Of course, there are always exceptions, but this distinction holds generally. While university education is more academic and includes diversified subjects to give students a more well-rounded education, college programs focus on specific subjects and are intended to train students to perform a specific job or to master a specific skill. Many colleges offer credits that can be transferred to a university program if the student wishes to upgrade their education to a university-level program.

Colleges are typically viewed as a good path for students who complete high school and wish to pursue a career-focused program that teaches

them specific skills for their target job. For example, colleges offer programs in cooking, law enforcement, automotive repair, construction, business, accounting, animation, dental assisting, design, paralegal, among others. As you will notice, these programs offer practical and career-focused training for doing specific jobs.

Universities offer more academic and general training emphasising critical thinking, analysis, and problem-solving. University programs are typically grouped into faculties, such as science, engineering, education, humanities, medicine, business and law. A student within the faculty of science can pursue a degree in chemistry, biology, or physics. University students also often have some freedom in selecting the courses they wish to pursue and are often required to take at least some courses from outside their faculty to ensure they are exposed to various subjects during their education.

Universities are viewed as academically more rigorous and the programs are more challenging, and therefore they have higher standards for accepting students. Many university programs are very competitive and only top students can achieve admission. Colleges have lower admission standards, and it's often easier to gain admission to college programs.

Universities and colleges are spread across Canada, and most cities have at least a community college. Therefore, it is important to have some understanding of Canada's geography and provinces to appreciate where the institutions are located. The following table shows a list of some universities and colleges in each province. The list is not exhaustive but gives an overview and appreciation of the spread of these institutions across Canada. There are many online resources that help international students find and choose an institution and study program, and that would have more comprehensive lists than what is provided below.

Selected Listing of Universities and Colleges in Western Canada		
Province	Selected Universities	Selected Colleges
British Columbia	University of British Columbia, Simon Fraser University, Royal Roads University, University of Victoria	Douglas College, British Columbia Institute of Technology, Camosun College, Langara College, Okanagan College
Alberta	University of Alberta, University of Calgary, Athabasca University	NorQuest College, Northern Alberta Institute of Technology, Red Deer College, Lethbridge College, Lakeland College, Bow Valley College
Saskatchewan	University of Regina, University of Saskatchewan	Saskatchewan Polytechnic
Manitoba	University of Manitoba, University of Winnipeg	Red River College

Selected Listing of Universities and Colleges in Central Canada		
Province	Selected Universities	Selected Colleges
Ontario	University of Toronto, University of Ottawa, Queen's University, Western University, McMaster University, University of Waterloo, Wilfrid Laurier University, Carleton University, Ryerson University, York University	Algonquin College, Centennial College, Conestoga College, Durham College, Fanshawe College, George Brown College, Humber College, La Cité collégiale, Seneca College
Prince Edward Island (PEI)	University of Prince Edward Island	Holland College
Quebec	McGill University, Concordia University, École Polytechnique de Montréal, HEC Montréal, Université de Montréal and Université du Québec à Montréal	CEGEP colleges, Vanier College, Collège Montmorency, Heritage College

Selected Listing of Universities and Colleges in Eastern Canada

Province	Selected Universities	Selected Colleges
New Brunswick	University of New Brunswick	New Brunswick Community College
Newfoundland and Labrador	Memorial University of Newfoundland	College of the North Atlantic
Nova Scotia	Dalhousie University, Saint Mary's University	Nova Scotia Community College
Prince Edward Island (PEI)	University of Prince Edward Island	Holland College

Selected Listing of Universities and Colleges in Northern Canada

Territory	Selected Universities	Selected Colleges
Northwest Territories	N/A	Aurora College
Yukon	Yukon University	Yukon School of Visual Arts
Nunavut	N/A	Nunavut Arctic College

Figure 3: Tulip Festival, Ottawa, Ontario, Canada [4]

International Students in Canada

Multiculturalism is widely accepted by Canadians as one of the key values of Canada. This means that Canadians don't expect everyone to conform to a single culture. Rather, Canadians welcome the diversity of different cultures that people bring from their home countries around the world.

---

[4] **Source:** Paul Shannon, CC BY-SA 2.5 <https://creativecommons.org/licenses/by-sa/2.5>, via Wikimedia Commons
https://commons.wikimedia.org/wiki/File:Garden_of_the_Provinces_and_Territories_-_Tulip_Festival_-_4.jpg

Many Canadians believe that this diversity of cultures, backgrounds, and opinions makes us stronger as a country. By taking the best of each culture, we can learn from the combined wisdom of many civilizations and cultures, and work on improving our own society.

This also means that we must respect cultural diversity. If everyone accepts the basic principles and laws of Canada and agrees to uphold them and to work within Canada's existing system, then it does not matter what language they speak in their home, what religion they practice, how they dress, or what foods they prefer to eat. This makes Canada a welcoming place for international students because they will almost always find communities of people from their own culture who can help them stay connected to their home country. No matter what religion you practice, or what your mother tongue is, you will likely find others with whom you can share your beliefs, language, festivals, and food!

Also, Canada's economic growth depends on attracting the best and brightest from around the world. Canada's immigration system brings in skilled workers and workers for occupations highly in demand in Canada. These workers contribute to Canada's economy by filling these jobs, which helps the companies that employ them to continue growing and being profitable. These workers also pay taxes and participate in the

Canadian economy by spending, saving and investing their salaries in Canada.

International students are an important source of new skilled workers for Canada. They are often good candidates for immigration to Canada because they are highly educated and are often the best students in their home countries. Also, by studying in Canadian institutions, these students gain a very clear understanding of life in Canada by the time they graduate, which makes their integration into Canadian society and Canada's economy much easier. For this reason, Canadian immigration policy welcomes international students.

According to the Canadian Bureau for International Education (CBIE)[5], there were over 600,000 international students at all levels in 2019. About half of all international students in Canada come from India and China. The rest come from all over the world, including South Korea, Vietnam, France, Iran, Nigeria, Brazil, and the USA, among others. The top destination for international students within Canada is Ontario, attracting nearly half of all students. British Columbia and Quebec come in second and third place, attracting nearly 40% of students, with the rest spread out among the remaining provinces.

---

[5] See: https://www.cbie.ca/

According to CBIE surveys, the top three reasons that international students cited for choosing Canada are the quality of Canadian education, Canada's reputation as a tolerant society, and Canada's reputation as a safe country. International students are overwhelmingly satisfied with their study experience in Canada, with 96% of those surveyed stating that they would recommend Canada as a study destination. Also, 60% of international students plan to apply for permanent residency and settle in Canada after completing their studies.

Advantages of Studying in Canada

In recent years, Canada has cemented its position as a top destination for students. In 2019, the number of international students in Canada had overtaken Australia. Only the USA, UK and China attract more international students than Canada. There are several reasons international students study in Canada.

Quality of Education

The quality of education obtained at Canadian post-secondary institutions is an important factor in attracting students. Canadian colleges and universities are well-resourced compared to those in most other countries worldwide. This translates into better access to labs, equipment, books, internet connectivity, and other resources that can

enrich the student experience. Also, many universities have significant research budgets that allow cutting-edge research programs to be carried out, which provides opportunities for graduate students to participate and gain experience working on globally leading research. This also means that professors at these universities are often at the top of their field, providing opportunities for students to learn from the top experts in their subjects.

Diversity and Multiculturalism

Canada's openness to diversity and multiculturalism is another attraction for international students, as it gives them a comfort level that they will be accepted and respected in Canada. Also, the diversity of the student body at Canadian universities enriches the learning experience. Students at Canadian universities will likely have classmates from many backgrounds. They will study and interact with each other, learn from their shared experiences, and build lasting connections, relationships, and friendships.

Safety

Safety is another important consideration. Relatively low crime rates and a feeling of personal safety make the student experience a pleasant one. Students can enjoy Canada, visit different cities and tourist attractions,

enjoy the local nightlife, and use public transportation without ever feeling they are in danger. Canada is also lucky to be free of any armed conflicts or deep political tensions, which translates into a more peaceful life for Canadians and international students.

Cost of Living and Tuition Fees

The cost of living and tuition fees are also another attraction for studying in Canada. Although international students pay higher tuition fees than Canadian students, the fees are still very reasonable and are often significantly lower than fees in other countries such as the United States. Also, the cost of living in most Canadian cities can be lower than other destinations. This makes Canada accessible to more students of various financial capabilities.

But why do international students pay higher tuition fees than local Canadian students? Many international students ask this question, and some may feel it is not fair or discriminatory. However, the reason for this is that Canadian governments at the federal and provincial levels provide funding to educational institutions to subsidize the costs for Canadian students to encourage and support more Canadians to seek higher education. The source of this funding is from taxes and fees collected by these governments from Canadians. This funding support translates into

lower fees for Canadian students. It would not be possible or fair for Canadians to subsidize the studies of students from around the world from their own tax money. Therefore, international students pay higher fees because they are new to Canada and have not yet contributed to Canada's tax system, at least not to the same extent as Canadian citizens who have lived and worked in Canada their entire lives.

Working During Studies and After Graduation

Another important reason international students study in Canada is the opportunity to work. Many international students receive permission to work while they study, which is indicated on their study permit. Depending on the situation, full-time students may be eligible to work on-campus without having to get a separate work permit. Also, full-time international students may be allowed to work off-campus for up to 20 hours a week during study sessions and full-time during scheduled study breaks and holidays, without having to get a separate work permit. When an internship or co-op work experience is required as part of a study program, international students may apply for a work permit to allow them to satisfy the requirements of their study programs[6]. All these possibilities for work allow students to get some work experience in

---

[6] Eligibility to work on-campus, off-campus, or for a co-op or internship is subject to certain conditions.

Canada while they study, and help them to get some income during their studies. Of course, international students must verify their eligibility according to the rules outlined by Immigration, Refugees and Citizenship Canada (IRCC) before starting work to ensure that they don't break the conditions of their study permit, which could lead to serious consequences.

After completing their study program, international students may also be eligible to apply for a Post-graduation work permit (PGWP)[7], which allows them to work for any employer anywhere in Canada for a certain period. The length of the PGWP depends on the length of study in Canada but could be up to three years. This allows international students to gain Canadian experience, which can be valuable for their careers. It also allows them to improve their chances of getting Canadian permanent residency.

Keeping the Family Together

International students with a valid study permit may apply for their spouses, common-law partners, and children to join them in Canada while they study. This is a great opportunity to help keep families together, and to allow students to have their immediate family with them

---

[7] Eligibility is subject to certain conditions.

in Canada as a support network while they study. Eligible family members can apply together with the main study permit applicant, or they can apply later to join the international student once they are in Canada.

Spouses or common-law partners of international students may be eligible to apply for an open work permit, which allows them to work for any employer. This can be very attractive for married / common-law couples because it allows the student's partner to work and gain work experience and support the couple financially during the period of studies in Canada.

Alternatively, spouses or common-law partners of international students in Canada can apply for visitor status if they do not intend to work while they are in Canada. Minor children are permitted to attend public Canadian primary and secondary schools as well, so the children of international students will have access to a great education during their time in Canada. The specific rules and regulations around minors attending public schools varies by province and school board, so students should investigate further before they arrive in Canada.

Pathway to Permanent Residency

Canada's system for selecting applicants for permanent residency rewards those who have studied or worked in Canada. Therefore, studying in

Canada offers international students a path towards applying for permanent residency in Canada and greatly improves their chances compared to those with no previous ties to Canada. Students who obtain permanent residency in Canada may then apply to become Canadian Citizens once they have fulfilled the requirements outlined by the IRCC.

All these reasons make Canada an attractive destination for international students. It is expected that the number of international students coming to Canada will continue to grow. This is especially true because while some other countries are moving to restrict and reduce the number of international students and make permanent residency and citizenship more difficult, Canada continues to welcome international students as a part of its overall immigration strategy.

Summary: Advantages of Studying in Canada
<ul><li>Quality of education</li><li>Diversity and multiculturalism</li><li>Safety</li><li>Cost of living and tuition fees</li><li>Work during studies and after graduation</li><li>Keeping the family together</li><li>Pathways to permanent residency</li></ul>

Figure 4: The Fairmont Empress, Victoria, British Columbia [8]

---

[8] **Source:** Dllu, CC BY-SA 4.0 <https://creativecommons.org/licenses/by-sa/4.0>, via Wikimedia Commons https://upload.wikimedia.org/wikipedia/commons/0/0d/The_Fairmont_Empress%2C_blue_hour.jpg

Case Study 1 - Choosing Canada

Huang had been dreaming about traveling to study abroad since he was in high school. Growing up in Singapore, his family was doing well financially, but they did not have many opportunities to travel. Huang always felt that he wanted to see other countries and explore the world. He liked adventures, and he wanted to meet new people and get to know other cultures.

In his last year of secondary school, Huang spent almost as much time exploring study abroad options as he did studying. Luckily, he was quite intelligent and had always done well in school. Huang loved computers and he knew he wanted to study computer science or engineering. He explored the possibility of studying in Australia. There are some very good universities there, and plus it would be close to home. He also looked at a few universities in the UK and in the USA.

Although he wanted to explore new cultures, Huang did not want to have to learn new languages, so he focused on English language universities. Then he came across the University of Waterloo in Canada. Not only did they have a very strong computer science program, but also the photos of the campus and the city of Waterloo were so beautiful.

Huang knew that Canada would be colder, but having lived in Singapore all his life, he never had a chance to see snow. He wanted to try skiing and skating, and Canada would be the perfect place for that! He also found out that the summers are incredibly warm and beautiful, and he could go hiking in the forest or canoeing in the river. The Canadian dollar is less expensive than the US dollar or British pound, and doing

some quick calculations, he found that it would be overall more affordable to study in Canada.

The decision was made! Huang got very excited about Canada, and started reading about it and looking at photos of Canada every day online. He also started to plan his university applications. Sure, he had to apply to some easy universities and colleges in Singapore as a backup plan. But his main goal was to study at the University of Waterloo.

After speaking with his parents, he felt even more confident. They told him that they have been saving for his education since he was born. They had the equivalent of $30,000 Canadian dollars to give him, which would cover a big chunk of his first year costs. He immediately downloaded the university application package, prepared everything, and submitted it.

To his great excitement, he received an admission offer! His dream was getting closer to reality, but he knew there were a few more steps he had to take. He studied all the laws and rules related to study permits. He prepared all of his documents, and then decided to hire an immigration consultant to answer some questions and review his documents. He knew this was the final step to achieve his dream.

One morning, he saw an email from the IRCC about an update related to his application. He opened the message, and his application was approved! He couldn't contain his excitement, and immediately started making his travel arrangements. Huang's dream had come true, and he was finally on his way to study abroad!

STEP 2: Getting Admission

Getting Admission to an Educational Institution in Canada

The previous chapters have provided an overview about Canada, its history, geography, political situation, and an overview of why international students study in Canada. This chapter will focus on the actual process of becoming a student in Canada. It is divided into subsections representing the steps that need to be followed. First, the right educational institution and program must be chosen. Then, the student must apply and gain admission to their chosen program. Once admission has been obtained, the student can then apply for a study permit, and only when the study permit is received can the student travel to Canada and begin their studies.

Finding the Right Institution And Program

The first step to studying in Canada is to identify the program or programs you would like to pursue. If you have completed an undergraduate degree and plan to pursue graduate studies in Canada, then the choice might be easier because you will most likely continue in the same field. If you are just completing secondary school, you may have a lot of options to choose from. In all cases, there are many factors to consider, and so here is a list of a few things to think about:

1) **Choose a program you love.** Most importantly, choose programs that are interesting to you. You will be more successful and motivated when studying a subject that truly engages you and that you really want to learn about. You will also be more successful in your career if you are doing something you love, rather than trying to force yourself to do something you don't really like to do very much.

2) **Know your own strengths.** Think deeply about the things that you are good at and the things you are not. Are you good at mathematics? Are you great at writing essays and laying out arguments? Do you have a deep understanding of science? Do you enjoy working with people? Are you a computer genius? This is not to say that you have to choose a program where you are strong. We can always grow and learn new things, and you may want to go in that direction and strengthen some areas that you have not been strong at before. This is OK, as long as you have thought about it and you know what you are getting into. Refer to Figure 5 to see one possible mental model you can use to find your passion and your life's purpose. It is known as Ikigai in Japanese. The idea is to find the intersection of what you love,

what you're good at, what the world needs, and what you can get paid to do!

3) **Understand career options and earning potential.** Do some research to discover what kinds of jobs the programs you are considering will most likely lead you to. Make sure you understand what those jobs entail and see if this is where you want to dedicate your career. Also, understand earning potential and average salaries in each field you are thinking about. While passion and loving what you do are important, earning enough money to enjoy a decent lifestyle is also an important consideration. Also, make sure you weigh the costs of pursuing an international education against the future earning potential you will have after graduation. This will help you to determine the "return-on-investment". In other words, how quickly will you be able to earn back the amount you spend on your education, and are you comfortable with making that investment?

4) **University/College Ranking and Reputation.** Not everyone has to go to a top school, and the top-ranked schools can be very hard to get into. Also, as you advance in your career, it is your experience that will define you more than which university you went to. Nonetheless, you should understand the ranking and reputation of

the educational institutions you are considering. There are some organizations that publish university and college rankings. You can also read reviews from other students or blog posts from graduates of a certain school to better understand their experience. You may even consider connecting with a former or current student directly through social media or your personal networks. Make sure you are comfortable with what you find out, and always look for more than one opinion before making any decisions.

5) **Location of the University or College.** Get information about the location of the universities and colleges you are considering. Which provinces are they in? What cities? Are they in the downtown area of a major metropolitan area, or is it a more rural setting in a smaller town? The location of where you will be living and studying will significantly impact your overall experience. There is no right or wrong answer, and different people will be attracted to different settings. Look at photos online of the campus and the city, and do some research to understand nearby attractions, transportation options, living costs, and weather.

6) **Understand the financial requirements.** To qualify for a study permit, you will need to prove that you have a financial plan to

pay your tuition fees and living expenses. Get information about the tuition fees and living expenses relevant to each program of interest. Think about your financial situation and see how much money you can put together. You may also have parents or close relatives who are willing to support you financially while you study. If required, consider whether you would qualify for an educational loan to help with the costs of your education. Put together a table breaking down all expected expenses including tuition fees and living costs. Then build another table adding up all available money sources, and make sure you can afford your education. Also, ask each institution about the possibility of getting scholarships or bursaries. Graduate programs may offer a guaranteed funding package in exchange for doing research/teaching assistantships.

7) **Visit the institution.** This is an optional step. Most students do not get the opportunity to visit the institution they are planning to study at before arriving to begin their studies, and most international students have never even been to Canada before starting their studies here! However, for those students who have the financial capability and can secure a visit visa to come to Canada, it is helpful to see the institution, take a tour, and get to

know the city you will be living in. Also, having a previous visit visa and travel history to Canada is helpful when applying for a study permit. Remember that a visa rejection could negatively affect future visa applications, including a study permit, so if you visit Canada make sure you understand the requirements and that you are confident that your visa application will be approved.

Figure 5: Ikigai - Finding your life's purpose [9]

---

[9] **Source:** Eugenio Hansen, OFS, CC BY-SA 4.0 <https://creativecommons.org/licenses/by-sa/4.0>, via Wikimedia Commons
https://commons.wikimedia.org/wiki/File:Diagramo_de_Ikigajo_-en.svg

Once you have collected information about the programs you may be interested in, it would be a good idea to select the top 5 - 10 options and put together a table with four columns. In the first column, list the name of the program. In the second column, write down some basic facts such as the length of the program, the cost, the location of the college or university, its ranking or reputation, etc. The third column lists the "pros" or advantages of choosing that program. Finally, in the fourth column, list the "cons" or disadvantages of choosing that program. Once you have all this information written down in front of you, it will become easier to make decisions. You can slowly eliminate options that are obviously not the best for you until you narrow it down to a shortlist of programs you want to apply to.

Summary: Factors to Consider When Choosing a Study Program
- Choose a program you love
- Know your strengths
- Understand career options and earning potential
- Consider University/College ranking and reputation
- Consider the location and setting of the university
- Understand the financial requirements
- Visit the university or college if you can

Applications and Admissions

The application process and admissions requirements and procedures are specific to each institution and sometimes even vary depending on the chosen program. Therefore, you must do some research to understand what is required. Typically, this information will be available on the website of the institution or program, or it will be sent by email upon submitting an inquiry about the program. However, the following is a list of some of the most common requirements you will need:

1) **Academic record.** This is your high school diploma and transcripts if you are applying for your first post-secondary program or your Bachelor/Master's degree and transcripts if you are applying for graduate studies. The top-rated universities are the most competitive and require high grades for admission. Universities require higher academic standards for admission than Colleges. Also, competitive programs such as engineering will typically require higher grades.

2) **Course Requirements.** Some programs require applicants to have taken certain pre-requisite courses before admission. For example, many engineering programs will require that students have taken some math and science courses to allow them to keep up with the

program. Graduate programs will usually require an undergraduate degree in the same or closely related field. Understand the requirements and take the required courses, if any, before applying for admission.

3) **Language Skills.** International students usually must prove proficiency in English (or French for programs offered in French) to gain admission. Some institutions will also offer English as a Second Language (ESL) courses that students can take upon arrival in Canada to help improve their skills before starting the formal study program. The most common English language tests accepted by universities are the TOEFL and IELTS exams.

4) **Essay.** Most programs will require that international students submit a written essay or statement of intent with their application. This is intended to assess the student's language proficiency and writing skills, but more importantly, to also assess their fit with the program. Colleges and universities want to ensure that the outcomes international students receive from their education will match their expectations and goals.

5) **Extracurricular and Volunteer Activities.** Besides academic achievement, some programs consider the extracurricular and

volunteer activities of applicants. This is especially important for competitive programs, where many students with high academic achievement will apply. Volunteer activities and community service, sports, music, clubs, and other activities outside of formal school work may be considered for admissions.

6) **References.** Some programs will ask for academic, professional, or personal references to be included with the admission application. This is particularly true for graduate programs and some professional programs. Many of these references can be completed online. However, it is the student's responsibility to get permission from their references before including their names and contact information in the admissions application.

7) **Admissions Tests.** Certain programs require specific test scores for admission. For example, business schools and especially MBA programs usually require GMAT scores and use them as a key consideration in making admissions decisions. The GRE is required for some graduate programs. Medical schools typically require the MCAT, while law schools require the LSAT.

Summary: Common Requirements for University Admissions
• Academic records • Course requirements • Language skills • Writing an essay • Extracurricular and volunteer activities • References • Admission tests

Case Study 2 - Admissions to a Master's Program

Saanvi grew up in a big family in Mumbai. She had two brothers and a sister, and she was the oldest of the four kids. Her parents owned a business and were quite successful. Although money was never an issue for the family, raising four children is still financially stressful. Saanvi had just graduated with a BSc in Chemistry 2 years ago from a local university. Her siblings would be going to university next over the coming years.

Knowing that she had to rely on herself financially if she ever wanted to go to graduate school, Saanvi has been working full time since graduation at a research lab close to her home. She was making a pretty good income for a new graduate. Luckily, because she still lived at home with her parents, she was able to save most of her income. Her parents were more than happy to have her live at home, especially since she was the math and science tutor at home!

But Saanvi was not satisfied with this life. She dreamed of becoming a professor and doing cutting edge research. She wanted to publish her findings and present her work at research conferences. Her boss at work was a senior research scientist, and she was constantly traveling to attend conferences and present her work. Saanvi knew that if she wanted to grow in the research field, she would need to get a graduate degree.

Saanvi had a cousin who went to Canada 5 years ago. He immigrated through express entry, and was now settled and working in Canada. He lived in Calgary, and although he sometimes complained about the weather, he was very happy overall. He was making a great income,

bought an apartment, and got married last year. He always encouraged her to think about immigrating to Canada as well.

She started to explore her immigration options, but she couldn't let go of her dream of advancing in the research field. So she decided to apply for Master's degrees in Canada. She applied to three different programs to be safe. She knew that admission was very competitive.

Saanvi spent 2 weeks preparing her application. She collected certified copies of her degree and transcripts, got two notarized reference letters from her professors, wrote essays about her motivations for studying a Master's degree in Chemistry and her dreams of being a professor and researcher. After many sleepless nights working on her applications, she finally submitted them!

Over the next few months, she started to receive responses. Her first choice, the University of Toronto, was not able to find her a spot that year. She was sad to hear this news. But then she got an admission offer to Western University, and started to celebrate! Two days later, she also got an admission offer to the University of Alberta.

The University of Alberta offer included a scholarship that would cover a lot of her costs. It was also located in Edmonton, which is close to her cousin who would only be a 3 hour drive away. She told her parents and siblings, and although they started crying because they knew they wouldn't see her for a long time, they were also celebrating because she was about to achieve her dreams!

Two years later, Saanvi graduated from the Master's degree and got admitted to the PhD program. She was well on her way to becoming Dr. Saanvi!

STEP 3: Getting a Study Permit

Getting a Study Permit

The biggest mistake that international students make regarding studying in Canada is that they don't take the study permit application seriously, because they believe that it is automatic once they receive admission to a university or college program. This is completely not true. Not paying close attention to the study permit application process and taking it for granted is the biggest reason for rejected applications which often means the student misses their opportunity to study in Canada.

Study permits are not granted automatically to international students when they receive admission to a Canadian school. Admission is required before applying for a study permit, but it does not guarantee that the study permit application will be approved. The student must ensure that they demonstrate their eligibility and meet all the requirements in their study permit application.

While study permit applications can often be submitted either online or by paper, it is highly encouraged that applicants submit their study permit applications through the online portal provided by Immigration, Refugees, and Citizenship Canada (IRCC). The online portal ensures faster processing, easier communication with the IRCC, and helps to ensure that all the required documents are attached before submission.

The study permit application process and requirements change from time to time. The specific requirements for study permit applications vary depending on the country the applicant is applying from. They also vary depending on the personal circumstances of the student. Therefore, it is not possible to cover the detailed requirements for every possible scenario in this book. Students should carefully read the information provided by the IRCC on their website to make sure they understand the process, and to ensure that they have the specific instruction guide and checklist that applies to them.

Rather than duplicating the instructions available on the IRCC web site, our goal in this book is to give you insights and strategies on how to approach your study permit application. We will offer you tips and tricks to maximize your chances of approval, and to avoid common mistakes that result in the refusal of study permit applications. We will help you to understand what the IRCC immigration officers are looking for when they examine study permit applications so that you can tailor your submission to answer their questions and address their concerns. But first, let's go through an overview of the process to help you better understand the formalities of the application process.

Overview of the process

The IRCC recommends that study permit applications be submitted through the online portal, rather than on paper. Paper applications are slowly being phased out, except for applicants who have special circumstances and must apply by paper.

The IRCC has provided online systems to facilitate the process of creating, submitting, and tracking your study permit application. While these systems are updated from time to time, the concept is generally the same. The first step is to find the link to the application portal on the IRCC web site. You will have to answer a few questions first, to indicate what type of application you want to submit, and where you are applying from. Based on your answers, you will be directed to create a portal account.

At the time of writing this book, there are two alternative portal systems that the IRCC uses. One is known as the "GCKey" portal. This is the older portal, and so requires that you download application forms as "fillable PDFs", complete them offline, and then re-upload them to the portal. The newer application portal, known simply as the "IRCC portal", is easier to use because the application forms are embedded in the portal and can be completed online instead of using fillable PDFs. The IRCC portal is being rolled out and will likely replace the GCKey portal at some point.

Regardless of which portal system you use, the process is generally the same. Once you enter the portal, you will be presented with a questionnaire to help determine your eligibility. The questionnaire will ask a series of standard questions about the student, their background, their family status, and what they are planning to do in Canada. Once completed, the system will show a checklist of the required application forms and supporting documents, and the applicable fees.

Another way to start your application is to use the "Come to Canada" online eligibility tool. It guides you through the questionnaire before you create a portal account. At the end of the questionnaire, you will see a checklist of required documents, and the required fees. It will also generate a personal reference code. You can then register a new account (or sign in to your account if you have already registered previously), select the option to apply for a study permit, and enter this personal reference code to load the checklist of documents that was previously generated.

Once you reach this point in the process, you will have a checklist of documents to complete and upload. If you are in the newer IRCC portal, you will complete the forms online through the portal. If you are in the older GCKey portal, you will download the fillable PDF forms, complete them on your local PC, and then re-upload them to the portal. In both

portals, you will also have to upload some supporting documents, such as a copy of your passport, a personal photo, your letter of acceptance, and proof of your financial ability to cover the costs of your program.

Once you complete the forms and upload all required supporting documents, you will be able to review your submission, and then you can proceed to pay the required fees. Finally, the application is submitted.

The applicant can log in to their account to stay updated with the progress of their application. The IRCC will send the applicant a message through the portal when further action is needed, such as when biometrics, a medical exam, or passport submission is required.

The exact steps, portal systems, and procedures for completing your application may vary slightly over time as the IRCC updates their systems. So you will need to visit the IRCC web site and follow the latest instructions and procedures. But with the overview discussed here, you will be prepared for what to expect.

For example, it is important to note that the Canadian visa application process does not require an in-person interview. Applications are processed based on the submitting documentation. Therefore, you should not count on having an opportunity to discuss your application with an immigration officer or to explain your circumstances. Rather, you

should make sure that the documentation that you upload and submit through the application portal is complete, and explains your situation accurately. Although in rare cases the applicant could be contacted by phone or asked for an in-person interview, these are rare exceptions. So before you start an application, make sure that you will be able to dedicate the time and effort required to gather the necessary documentation. It is also recommended that you have access to a high quality scanner so that you can provide clear copies of your documents.

Student Direct Stream (SDS)

The study permit process has two streams that applications can be processed under. The Student Direct Stream (SDS) has more strict requirements and requires more documentation to be submitted with your application than the regular stream, but benefits from faster processing. The SDS is also only available to students from certain countries.

At the time of writing, students who are legal residents of one the following countries were eligible for the SDS stream:

- Antigua and Barbuda
- Brazil
- China
- Colombia
- Costa Rica
- India
- Morocco
- Pakistan
- Peru
- Philippines
- Senegal
- Saint Vincent and the Grenadines
- Trinidad and Tobago
- Vietnam

The application portal will determine whether you are eligible for the regular or the SDS stream. Your answers to the application questionnaire will determine which stream you are eligible to apply under. If you meet all of the eligibility criteria of the SDS stream, your application will be processed under the SDS.

The SDS stream requirements include the following:

- Be a legal resident and live in one of the eligible countries.
- Have an acceptance letter from a post-secondary designated learning institution (DLI)
- Most recent secondary or post-secondary school transcript(s)
- Meeting minimum language test scores

- Proof of payment of the full tuition fees for your first year of study
- A Guaranteed Investment Certificate (GIC) of $10,000 Canadian dollars
- If planning to study in Quebec, you must have a Québec Acceptance Certificate (CAQ)
- Medical exam completed prior to applying (if you need one)
- Police certificate (if you need one)

If you meet all of the criteria above and the system determines that you are eligible for the SDS, then you will be informed that you are applying under the SDS. Otherwise, you will submit a study permit application that will be processed in the regular stream. Other than the higher level of requirements and faster processing in the SDS, the rest of the process is the same as the regular study permit process.

General Requirements

While the specific requirements may change from time to time and depend on the country the applicant is applying from, the following are some general requirements that are often applicable.

> a) **Form IMM1294 - Application for Study Permit Made Outside of Canada.** This is the main application form where the applicant will enter their personal details,

information about the program they are applying for, and answer questions about their personal history to determine their eligibility.

b) **Form IMM5645 or IMM5707 - Family Information.** This form is used to submit information about the applicant's family members. Make sure you read the form and instructions carefully, as these forms can be confusing. Complete all required information and don't forget to sign all required sections, as applicable to your personal circumstances.

c) **Letter of Acceptance.** The educational institution provides the letter of acceptance to the applicant. The letter is proof the student has received admission. The letter should indicate the program name, start and end dates, and tuition costs at a minimum. The Designated Learning Institution (DLI) number of the institution should also be included, especially for smaller and less well-known institutions.

d) **Passport and Digital Photo.** When uploading a copy of your passport, the main information and signature pages

are required. Applicants are also strongly advised to include all pages with stamps or visas on them, as showing a successful travel history can help with the study permit application. A digital photo is also required. Typically, a passport photo is sufficient, but there are specific requirements and it is advised to make sure the photo you submit meets the requirements to avoid any problems.

e) **Proof of Financial Support.** This section should include documents proving that the student can meet the financial requirements of their study in Canada. The student should generate a budget showing tuition plus living expenses and then list their funding sources to prove that they can cover the costs. Students must prove that they have sufficient funds to cover at least the first year of their studies. Funding sources can include personal funds, scholarships, loans, and support letters from parents or close relatives. Bank statements going back at least four months are required to prove availability of funds. Support letters and bank statements are required if support from parents or relatives is required, as well as evidence proving the relationship.

f) **Letter of Explanation.** This letter acts as a cover letter for the entire application. Here, the student should describe their background, why they are interested in studying in Canada, why they selected this specific program and institution, and what they plan to do after completing their studies and returning to their home country. This should provide logical reasoning to prove that you are a legitimate student planning to come to Canada to study. The letter of explanation should also include a breakdown of the finances to prove that you can cover the costs of your education. Prior travel history, letters of recommendation from work, prior degrees and transcripts, English language test scores, and any other relevant supporting documents can also be attached to the letter of explanation. Please note that in the application portal, you will not see a section labelled "Letter of Explanation". In the GCKey portal, you can upload your Letter of Explanation along with all its attachments in the section called "Client Information", which you will find marked as optional. In the IRCC portal, you can upload it under "Additional Information". Although the application portals treat this optional, it is highly recommended.

g) **Medical and Police.** Medical exams are required in some circumstances depending on the reason for visiting Canada and the country from which the applicant is coming. If required, the applicant has the choice of doing the medical prior to submitting their application or waiting until it is requested by the IRCC. The medical must be performed by an approved physician. Details on medical exams are available on the IRCC website. In addition, police background checks are required for applicants from some countries. Details on police checks are also available on the IRCC website.

h) **Applications for Family Members.** As part of the questionnaire while applying for a study permit, the applicant will have the opportunity to include applications for family members. For example, the applicant can apply for an open work permit for their spouse at the same time as they apply for their study permit. The additional applications will require their own forms and documents and will incur additional fees.

i) **CAQ for Quebec.** If the university you are applying for is in the province of Quebec, you must obtain a Québec

Acceptance Certificate (CAQ) for studies before you apply for your study permit. There is a separate process to obtain a CAQ, as well as additional fees. Take this into account as you prepare for your study permit application. If your university is not in Quebec, then you do not need the CAQ.

Summary: Study Permit Requirements
- Form IMM1294 (Application for Study Permit)
- Form IMM5645 or IMM5707 (Family Information)
- Letter of acceptance
- Copy of your passport
- Digital photo
- Proof of financial support
- Letter of explanation
- Medical exam
- Police clearance letter
- CAQ (for Quebec institutions)
- Application forms and supporting documents for accompanying family members

Key Considerations

Remember that a significant proportion of study permit applications are rejected, even though the applicants have received admission to a Canadian college or university. Even students accepted into the top universities and the most competitive and prestigious programs have had their study permit applications denied. Therefore, it is important to craft your application carefully to demonstrate to the IRCC that you meet all the eligibility requirements. Demonstrate that you are a legitimate student, that you intend to only stay in Canada temporarily to study, and that you have the financial capability to pay your costs. Use your letter of explanation to provide a clear and easy-to-follow narrative to show all these points, and use supporting documents as evidence for every claim you make.

Figure 6: Parliament Buildings, Ottawa [10]

---

[10] **Source:** Saffron Blaze, CC BY-SA 3.0 <https://creativecommons.org/licenses/by-sa/3.0>, via Wikimedia Commons https://commons.wikimedia.org/wiki/File:Centre_Block_-_Parliament_Hill.jpg

Tips & Tricks

The following are some helpful tips and tricks to help you avoid easy mistakes and to help make your application as strong as possible.

1. **Apply as early as possible**

   Use the IRCC's online "Check Processing Times" tool to get an estimate of how long an average study permit takes to process, but don't fully trust it. The processing times change depending on the time of year. The IRCC's workload also impacts the average processing time. For example, the COVID19 pandemic resulted in significant delays and created a large backlog of applications. For some types of applications, the IRCC's tool also allows you to find the processing time specific to the country where you are applying from.

   Keep in mind that the processing time cited by the tool is an average, which means that half the applications will likely take longer. It is also based on the processing times of past applications, and so it does not take into account future increases in case load.

   Use the tool to get an idea of the timelines, and reset your expectations about how long the process will take. Many students

start with the assumption that the study permit is something they can take care of a few weeks before they intend to travel, but using the tool they will find out that it takes weeks or months to receive an approval. Once you are aware of the rough timeline to expect, make sure you add a few weeks to the timeline to give yourself extra time in case you encounter longer than normal processing, or in case a re-application is necessary.

2. Get the list of requirements for your country

The IRCC web site includes a tool that allows you to download "visa office instructions", which are application instructions for each specific country. These instructions are typically intended for paper applications, because the online application portal presents you with its own set of requirements and a checklist of documents to upload. It is always recommended to apply online whenever possible, because that facilitates the application process and can make the process faster overall.

Keep in mind that applying through the Student Direct Stream (SDS) also typically requires you to follow the requirements outlined in the country specific visa office instructions. So if you

are applying through the SDS, you should adhere to the instructions in the visa office instructions.

Even if you are applying online through the regular study permit application stream, it is still a good idea to review the visa office instructions for your country and incorporate any special requirements in your application. For example, some countries will request police reports and have special instructions for how to obtain them. Other countries request language test results, or have specific instructions for how to provide proof of means of financial support. Some countries may require other country-specific documentation, such as tax return documents.

If you provide these special requirements, you will have done your best to answer any potential questions that may arise during the processing of your application. This should lead to faster processing time and boost your chances of receiving an approval.

3. **Take your time**

A Canadian study permit application is not intended to be something that you do in a couple of hours during your free time. It is not a straightforward process where you just have a few

simple forms that you fill in and submit. There is a lot more to it than that!

Take your time to understand the requirements, collect required documents, get extra supporting documentation, organize everything and label it well, anticipate any questions the officer may ask and try to answer them clearly and with supporting documentation.

It's recommended that you start the study permit application process as soon as you receive your letter of acceptance from the university or college you are applying to. Make a checklist of what needs to be done, and how long each item will take. This will help you to stay on track and avoid any surprises. For example, if you are applying for a loan to cover some of your expenses, then you need to take into account that the process to apply and receive a loan approval letter may take a few weeks. Also, if you need support from family members, you will need time to obtain bank statements and a signed letter of support. English language testing may take a few weeks for you to register, prepare, write the test, and receive the test results. If your university is in Quebec, it will take you a few weeks to obtain the CAQ for studies.

Keep all these factors in mind and start the process early. Track your progress to ensure that you stay on track and that you are ready to apply within the expected timeframes.

4. **Check if a Medical Examination or Police Report is required**

People who intend to visit Canada temporarily may be required to undergo a medical examination as part of their application process. For study permit applicants who plan to stay in Canada longer than 6 months, a medical examination is required for applicants who have lived in a 'designated' country for at least 6 months in a row within the last year.

The list of designated countries is published on the IRCC web site. Make sure you check this early to confirm whether you will need a medical exam or not, and give yourself enough time to schedule the doctor visit.

When a medical exam is required, you have two options to complete it. You can do an "upfront" medical exam before applying. This will speed up the process, because it allows you to include the medical information form with your application. Assuming everything else in your application looks good, the officer will be able to verify your medical and move quickly to

approving your application. The other option is for you to submit a complete application without doing the medical examination upfront. In this case, if the rest of your application is found to meet the eligibility criteria, you will receive a letter in the application portal requesting that you complete the medical exam. You will then have to take an appointment, perform the exam, and then upload the medical information form to the portal to allow the processing of your application to be completed.

You are responsible for the costs of the medical examination, and this will vary depending on the country where you are applying. This is why some applicants choose not to do an upfront medical examination, because if they are found not eligible for a study permit and they receive a refusal, the costs of doing the medical exam will be wasted. If cost is a concern for you and you choose not to do the medical exam upfront, keep in mind to add a couple of weeks to the expected processing time of your application to account for the pause in processing while you perform the medical exam.

Police reports are less frequently required for study permit applicants. As mentioned previously, some countries request police reports to be submitted, and this is indicated in the

country-specific visa instructions. In other cases, you may receive a request for a police report during processing of your application. Depending on the country, sometimes police reports are complicated to obtain, or the process takes a long time. So it's a good idea to research all the countries you have lived in to understand the requirements for getting a police certificate, the process, and how long it takes. It's good to know early whether you need them, and if so, start the process to get them to avoid any unnecessary delays.

5. **Include evidence of English or French language proficiency**

If you are applying under the SDS stream, you are required to prove your language proficiency by providing one of the approved language examination results. Also, some countries require language examination results in their "visa office instructions". So make sure to follow those instructions if applicable. Check the IRCC web site for the latest information about acceptable examinations.

Even if language examination results are not strictly required in your case, proving that you are fluent in the language of instruction of your intended study program is an easy way to avoid

a commonly cited reason for refusal. This is best done with one of the language exams recognized by the IRCC.

If you can't do an examination, then try to provide other evidence that you will be successful in the program and that language will not be a barrier for you. For example, if you are going to study in English, then think of ways you can convince the officer that you are fluent enough to study in English. Did you have to write a TOFEL exam? Did you do any previous studies or work in English? Did you have to write any essays or do interviews in order to get acceptance into your chosen program? Or do you plan on joining an ESL program before starting your formal studies? Any and all of these could be used to prove that language will not be a problem for you.

6. **Pay special attention to your proof financial support**

One of the requirements of a study permit application is the "proof of financial support" documentation. In order to be eligible to study in Canada, you have to prove that you are able to cover the costs of your tuition fees, living expenses, and any other costs during your studies.

Ideally, you should show that you have access to enough money for the entire duration of your program. This will greatly increase your chances of receiving an approval for your study permit application. If this is difficult, at a minimum you must show that you can cover the tuition fees and living expenses of the first year of studies. But you should also provide some discussion of how you will finance the remainder of the duration of your studies. For example, do you have a source of income that will help you save money to cover the costs of the remaining years? Or if you are getting support from your parents, do they have income that they can set aside? Make some calculations and explain your plan to the officer to convince them that you will not run out of money while you are in Canada.

So how can you show that you have enough money? Start by building a table showing the total expenses that you will need during your stay in Canada. Make sure to include tuition fees, any other ancillary fees due to your educational institution, the cost of flights to and from Canada, and living expenses including rent, food, utilities, bills, entertainment, and other miscellaneous items. The total sum of these expenses will be your target.

The second step is to create a table showing your sources of funds. This could include scholarships, deposit payments, loans, personal funds, and support from parents or other family members. For each item on this list, you will need to attach the required evidence that these funds exist, are liquid, and are available to use when needed. The total available funds should exceed or at the very least equal the total expense amount you calculated. If you are getting support from your parents, you will need to provide a signed support letter indicating the amount of money they will be contributing towards your education. You will also need to provide evidence of your relationship, such as a birth certificate.

7. **Keep an eye out for the Biometrics request letter**

Within a day or two of submitting your application, you will receive a biometrics request letter. Make sure you monitor your email and the application portal closely to make sure you receive the letter without delay.

Read the letter carefully and follow the instructions to complete the biometrics process as quickly as possible to avoid delaying your application. Any delays in completing the biometrics are

above and beyond the normal processing times. In other words, the processing time cited by the IRCC does not start until your biometrics are submitted.

The biometrics appointment consists of taking your photo and fingerprints, and is typically carried out at a visa application center (VAC). Find the list of visa application centers on the IRCC web site. The processes and instructions vary by country, so make sure you follow the instructions specific to your VAC. You will normally have to take an appointment, and you will be instructed to bring the biometrics request letter and your passport to your appointment. However, it is possible that some VACs may allow walk-ins or have other processes.

8. **Don't arrive in Canada too early**

Your study permit application is intended to be used to allow you to travel to and reside in Canada for the purpose of pursuing your educational program. You are not allowed to work before the start of your program. Also, you will have typically calculated your living expenses budget to account for the duration of your study program.

If you arrive in Canada too early before the start of your program, you will raise questions about what you intend to do in Canada during this time. Will you try to work illegally? Will your budget be enough to cover the expenses of this extra stay in Canada?

To avoid raising any questions, plan to arrive no more than 30 days prior to the official start date of your study program, as stated in your formal letter of acceptance. It is understood that you will need some time to find accommodations and get ready to start studying. But anything more than 30 days will raise unnecessary questions about your intentions.

9. Be very careful to avoid misrepresentation

The IRCC takes any attempt to mislead immigration officers very seriously. It is very important that you are honest and transparent in your application. Submitting false information or lying on an application can lead to serious consequences, including:

- Not being allowed to enter Canada for at least 5 years
- Having a permanent record of fraud with the Canadian government
- Losing your status as a permanent resident or Canadian citizen

- Being charged with a crime
- Removal from Canada

According to the IRCC web site[11]:

> It's a serious crime to lie, or to send false information or documents to Immigration, Refugees and Citizenship Canada (IRCC). This is fraud. It's called "misrepresentation."

> If you lie on an application or in an interview with an IRCC officer, this is also fraud. It's a crime.

Most students do not intentionally lie or falsify documents when applying to a study permit. However, sometimes students make mistakes in their application that could be viewed as misrepresentation. The most common example of this is omitting to mention previous visa refusals. The study permit application form clearly asks whether the applicant has ever received a visa refusal, and some students don't pay attention to this question or

---

[11] IRCC web site page on misrepresentation (as on November 14, 2022): https://www.canada.ca/en/immigration-refugees-citizenship/services/protect-fraud/document-misrepresentation.html

forget about a previous visa refusal. This is usually detected and considered an attempt to mislead the IRCC.

If you have a prior visa refusal, be transparent and mention it in your application. You can also explain the situation. For example, if you were refused due to lack of funds, or due to an unclear purpose for your visit, then you can mention this in your application. Although prior visa refusals can impact your application, your best course of action is to be transparent about them. Do not be tempted to misrepresent yourself because the consequences can be quite severe.

Another common source of misrepresentation is when applicants submit false or altered documents, and present them as original and official documents. Although it is easy these days to modify documents using computer software, doing so is a form of fraud and it can be detected. This is considered misrepresentation because the applicant is trying to mislead the immigration authorities by presenting altered documents.

Once again, students rarely intend to falsify documents. But sometimes they are tempted to adjust a document thinking that they are making it more clear. Another scenario to be careful of is

with documents in your original language. Sometimes students will be tempted to generate English versions of these original documents with the intention of helping the visa officers. However, it is not allowed to submit documents that you generated or altered and present them as original and official documents. There is a process for translation of documents that must be followed.

10. Translate your documents

Any supporting documents that you submit to the IRCC with your study permit application must be either in English or French, or must be translated to English or French. Translations must be done by a certified translator. A certified copy of the original must be provided, and accompanied by the certified translation.

The certified translator must be accredited or officially recognized or authorized in the country where the translation is being completed. They will confirm their certification by a seal or stamp that shows the translator's membership number of a professional translation association.

It is important to note that translations may not be done by the applicant, a member of the applicant's family, or the applicant's

lawyer or immigration consultant, whether they are certified translators or not.

In rare circumstances when a certified translator cannot be found, another translator can be used as long as they submit an affidavit where they swear that their translation is an accurate representation of the contents of the original document. The translator must sign the affidavit in front of a commissioner authorized to administer oaths in the country where they live, such as a lawyer or notary public.

Make sure that you take into account the timing and costs required to get translations of your supporting documents as you plan your study permit application.

Summary: Tips and Tricks

- Apply as early as possible
- Get the list of requirements for your country
- Take your time
- Check if a Medical Examination or Police Report is required
- Include evidence of English or French language proficiency
- Pay special attention to your proof financial support
- Keep an eye out for the Biometrics request letter
- Don't arrive in Canada too early
- Be very careful to avoid misrepresentation
- Translate your documents

Figure 7: Vancouver, British Columbia [12]

Bringing your Family

When completing the questionnaire to determine eligibility for a study permit, you will be asked if you want to apply for family members to join you during your stay in Canada. Only spouses, common-law partners, and dependent children are eligible to apply to come to Canada with you. Upon answering "yes" to this question, you will get the opportunity to

---

[12] **Source:** David G. Gordon, CC BY-SA 4.0 <https://creativecommons.org/licenses/by-sa/4.0>, via Wikimedia Commons
https://commons.wikimedia.org/wiki/File:Concord_Pacific_Master_Plan_Area.jpg

include applications for your family members which will be submitted at the same time as your study permit application.

Spousal Open Work Permits

If you have a spouse or common-law partner accompanying you to Canada, you have the option to apply for a visitor status or an open work permit for them to join you while you are in Canada. If your spouse or common-law partner intends to work in Canada, they should apply for the open work permit. If they do not intend to work, they can apply for visitor status. The visitor visa is less expensive than an open work permit, and so if your spouse is sure that they don't want to work, or if they will be staying at home to take care of young children, then a visitor visa may be the right choice.

However, in most cases applying for an open work permit is the right choice. Although the fees are slightly higher, the difference is not that significant given all the other costs of studying in Canada. At the time of this writing, a visitor visa carries a fee of $100 Canadian dollars, while an open work permit requires fees of $255 Canadian dollars (comprising a $155 work permit fee and a $100 open work permit holder fee).

Holding an open work permit does not mean that your spouse is required to work. Because it is an open work permit, they are not required to have

a job offer. They can arrive in Canada, and take their time to settle in. They can then choose to work for any employer, and they can choose if they want to work full-time or part-time. If they lose their job or decide to quit, there are no consequences on their open work permit. This flexibility makes the open work permit incredibly valuable.

Furthermore, getting professional work experience in Canada could be helpful if you or your spouse plan to apply for permanent residency in the future. Canadian work experience can add points to your CRS score, which is the scoring system used to select permanent residence applicants in Canada. It can also open the doors to other permanent residency application routes that are not otherwise available. For example, the Canada Experience Class permanent residency program is open to those who have at least 1 year of skilled work experience in Canada (or an equal amount of part-time work experience) in the 3 years before you apply.

Another advantage of obtaining an open work permit for your spouse or common-law partner is of course financial. The costs of studying in Canada can add up, especially if the student is dedicated to their studies and unable to work. Without an income, it can be hard to manage, and the financial stress and anxiety can take a toll. Having a spouse who has

an open work permit and who can work to contribute financially to support the family can provide a lot of relief.

If you choose to apply for an open work permit for your spouse or common-law partner at the same time as you apply for your study permit, the applications are typically processed concurrently. This means that when you get your study permit approval, your spouse will get their open work permit approval at the same time. This facilitates the ability to travel to Canada together.

On the other hand, some students choose to obtain their study permit and travel to Canada alone in the beginning to get settled. This is also an option, and you can apply for your spouse to join you later on, as they will continue to be eligible to apply for an open work permit as long as you are on a valid study permit in Canada.

Visitor Visas

You are also eligible to apply for visitor visas for your accompanying family members. This applies to both your spouse or common-law partner, or minor children.

As discussed in the previous section, for spouses you have the option to apply for either an open work permit or a visitor visa. Applying for a visitor visa incurs slightly lower application fees, but it limits your spouse

as they will not be able to work or register in formal education while they are on visitor status. A visitor visa can be the right choice if you have young children who will require full-time care by your spouse, and they will not have the opportunity to work anyway. Also, sometimes your spouse may want to just focus on helping you transition to Canada and manage your home life to minimize your stress so you can focus on your studies.

With a visitor visa, your spouse can of course live in Canada, tour your city, province or even the whole country, and even register for short general interest or language courses. Spouses remain eligible to apply for an open work permit at any time while you are still holding a valid study permit, even if they originally entered Canada as a visitor. So if they change their mind and decide to work, they can apply for an open work permit while they are in Canada. However, they may not start working until they receive the work permit.

Minor Children and Schooling

If you have minor children who will accompany you to Canada, you will typically apply for visitor visas for them as well. Minor children are permitted to attend public Canadian primary and secondary schools as well, so the children of international students will have access to a great

education during their time in Canada. The specific rules and regulations around minors attending public schools varies by province and school board, so students should investigate further before they arrive in Canada.

Maintaining a Valid Status

An important note for any temporary resident in Canada is that it is your responsibility to ensure that you maintain a valid status in Canada. Your study permit, or your family's work permits or visitor visas may expire earlier than you expect for some reasons. For example, visas often expire when the visa holder's passport expires. Make sure you keep a close eye on the expiry dates of visas and permits, to ensure that you always maintain a valid status in Canada. Overstaying beyond the expiry date of your status can cause complications, so it is easiest to avoid these issues by being diligent about tracking expiry dates, and applying for extensions or for new visas or statuses as necessary to maintain a valid status for the entire time that you are in Canada.

Hire a professional

As you can probably tell by now, applying for a study permit is not straightforward. Although there is a lot of information online, much of it is outdated or wrong. The IRCC provides guides on applying, but these

can be hard to understand and follow for someone who has never done it before. Therefore, it is always advisable to use the services of a lawyer or a Regulated Canadian Immigration Consultant (RCIC) to help guide you through applying for a study permit, or any other immigration-related application.

Approvals and Refusals

Now that you have learned about study permits and the application process for obtaining one, we will turn our attention to the possible outcomes of the process. The reality of the system is that there are two possible outcomes to a study permit application. The outcome that we hope for is a study permit approval. The other possibility is that the study permit application is refused. We will discuss study permit refusals and strategies to deal with a refusal in a dedicated section later on.

If a study permit application is approved, the applicant will receive a letter through the online portal (if they applied online) requesting that their passport be submitted to the nearest visa application center (VAC). A temporary residence visa will be stamped into the passport (if required). For students from countries where a visa is not required, an eTA will be issued instead. Besides the visa or eTA, the applicant will also receive a letter of introduction. Upon entering Canada, this letter will

show that a study permit has been approved. The study permit will then be issued to the student if the border services officers are satisfied that the student still meets the eligibility requirements.

Get To Know Your Study Permit

We have discussed applying for a study permit in quite some detail, but it is important to take a few moments to ensure that you understand what a study permit is. Many international students confuse the study permit with their study visa, and it is not always clear what the difference between these two concepts is.

Visa vs. eTA

First, it's important to clarify that foreign nationals who want to travel to Canada need to obtain either a visa or an eTA (Electronic Travel Authorization). Only US citizens or permanent residents (green card holders) may travel to Canada without obtaining prior authorization. So unless you are a US citizen or permanent resident, you should review the most updated visa requirements to confirm whether you will need a visa or an eTA to travel to Canada.

As a general overview, as of 2022, citizens of most European countries, Australia, New Zealand, Japan, South Korea, Taiwan, Mexico, Chile, and the UAE are exempt from requiring a visa to travel to Canada. They must

instead obtain an Electronic Travel Authorization (eTA) to board a flight to Canada. You can apply for an eTA online, and you will receive your approval by email. The eTA will be linked to your passport and will be visible when you attempt to board a flight to Canada. An eTA is not required if entering Canada by land or sea.

Citizens of most other countries in Africa, Asia, and South America are required to obtain a visa prior to traveling to Canada. A visa is typically stamped into your passport.

A visa or eTA is the document that authorizes you to travel to Canada, but it does not guarantee that you will be allowed entry. The Canadian border services officers will assess your eligibility to enter Canada at the point of entry and make the final determination.

As an international student, you do not need to apply for a visa or eTA separately. To make the process easier for international students, the IRCC will automatically grant a visa or eTA to study permit applicants when their applications are approved. Therefore, you only need to follow the study permit application process.

When/Where is a study permit issued?

You may be wondering: "If a study permit is not the same as a visa, then when will I receive my study permit?" This is a great question! When you

complete the study permit application process and submit your application, the IRCC will evaluate your application and determine whether you meet the eligibility requirements. If your application is approved, you will be granted a visa or eTA, and you will receive a "letter of introduction" in your application portal.

The letter of introduction will indicate that you have been approved for a study permit. It will also indicate the validity dates of the letter, which is the date by which you need to enter Canada to obtain your study permit. Make sure that you bring the letter of introduction with you when you travel to Canada. We will discuss what other documentation you need to bring in a later section of this book.

Upon arrival in Canada, the border services officer will assess your eligibility to enter Canada and to receive a study permit. If no issues are identified that would prevent your entry to Canada, you will then be issued your study permit at the point of entry in Canada. Make sure to verify that all information on the permit is correct before leaving the immigration officer, and ask for corrections to be made if you discover any mistakes.

What information is on the study permit?

The study permit itself will be printed on a separate sheet, and is not attached to your passport. It is printed on an official government of Canada document format with security features that help to ensure the document is authentic.

At the top of the study permit, you should see your name and permanent address. When you receive your study permit, review it to make sure your name is spelled correctly and that there are no typographical errors. The application number and your UCI number will also be printed at the top of the study permit document.

The main part of the document includes the study permit details, which includes your personal information such as your family name, given name, date of birth, gender, country of birth, country of citizenship and passport number. Below that is a section with additional information such as the study permit's date of issue, expiry date, name of your institution and field of study.

Below the main part of the study permit document, you will find the conditions of your study permit. This includes the date when you must leave Canada, conditions about the types of employment that you may pursue during your studies, and any other conditions attached to your

study permit. Make sure you read and understand these conditions, as you must abide by them in order to maintain a valid status in Canada. When you receive your study permit, make sure that the employment conditions are written in this section. Otherwise, you may not be eligible to work during your studies.

The study permit may also contain other remarks at the bottom of the page. These typically reiterate or further explain some of the conditions of your study permit. A note at the very bottom of the page reminds you that a study permit does not authorize re-entry to Canada. In other words, if you travel outside of Canada and then want to return, you must have a valid visa or eTA to re-enter Canada even if you have a valid study permit. The study permit in and of itself does not authorize you to travel to or enter Canada, and must be accompanied by a visa or eTA.

Key Dates on the Study Permit

The key date on your study permit that you need to keep in mind is the expiry date. This is the date when your status as a student in Canada will expire. You may not stay in Canada beyond this date. If your study program extends beyond the expiry date of your study permit, or if you extend your studies or wish to remain in Canada, you must apply for an extension of your status before the expiry date on your study permit.

It is your responsibility to ensure that you don't stay in Canada without a valid status. It is very important to always maintain a valid status in Canada. So make sure to keep the expiry date of your study permit in mind, and apply for an extension if needed at least 30 days before the expiry of your study permit.

The issue date listed on your study permit is less important, because it will typically be on the date that you arrive in Canada. So for most students, there is usually no risk that you will start studying before this date. Nonetheless, keep in mind that you should not start your study program before this date because your study permit is not valid until the issue date.

Study Permit Conditions

As discussed previously, you will find the conditions of your study permit listed below the main sections of the study permit document. The most important condition to keep in mind is the date when you must leave Canada. This should coincide with the expiry date of your study permit. It is your responsibility to either leave Canada before this date, or apply for an extension or change of status at least 30 days before the expiry of your study permit.

Another important condition that should be listed is related to the allowed employment during your studies. You should check your study permit when you receive it and verify that the types of employment you are allowed to pursue are outlined. If there is no mention of employment, you should ask the officer if they could add the employment conditions to your study permit to ensure that you have the option to work if you want to. Of course, the final decision is with the officer and they may have reasons to decline to grant you the authorization to work during your studies.

Typically, the employment condition should indicate that you are allowed to work on or off campus, as long as you are eligible to do so. The eligibility criteria and number of hours of work that you are allowed may vary, so make sure you check the latest information before you consider working.

Study Permit Refusals

Receiving a refusal on your study permit application can be heartbreaking and disappointing. You may question what you did wrong? You may even start to lose hope about studying in Canada. However, it is important to note that many students receive a refusal on study permit applications. Although it is not the outcome that we aim for, it is not completely

unusual. It is also not necessarily a final outcome. In this chapter, we will discuss what you can do if you have received a study permit refusal.

Study Permit Refusal Rates

Before we start discussing your options for responding to a study permit application refusal, let's take a look at the study permit approval rates for the years 2019 - 2021. This will allow you to adjust your expectations accordingly. The data is sourced from the government of Canada. The full data set is presented in the appendix, but below is a summary of refusal rates globally and among selected countries.

The data shows that globally, around 60% of study permit applications are approved. Conversely, this means that 40% of applications are refused. This aggregate number is quite high, but as you will notice while browning through the table, the number varies widely based on the country of residence of the applicant.

For example, in 2021, only 10% of study permit applications from residents of Afghanistan were approved. On the other hand, 99% of applications from residents of Japan were approved. Many other countries fall somewhere in between. So why is there such a stark difference in the approval rates between countries?

Study Permit Approval Rates from 2019 - 2021							
Country of Residence	2019	2020	2021	Country of Residence	2019	2020	2021
Global	**60%**	**51%**	**60%**	Iran	44%	46%	39%
Afghanistan	8%	8%	10%	Ireland	93%	82%	94%
Algeria	23%	15%	19%	Italy	92%	97%	95%
Argentina	87%	78%	74%	Japan	96%	98%	99%
Australia	88%	86%	83%	Mexico	81%	81%	87%
Bangladesh	42%	37%	46%	Myanmar	72%	75%	42%
Belgium	88%	94%	92%	New Zealand	87%	93%	86%
Bolivia	74%	59%	82%	Nigeria	17%	18%	34%
Brazil	83%	61%	80%	Norway	88%	96%	85%
Bulgaria	78%	83%	83%	Pakistan	29%	33%	37%
Cambodia	60%	75%	70%	Palestine	23%	25%	16%
Chile	82%	91%	91%	Peru	74%	67%	78%
China	85%	81%	84%	Philippines	62%	50%	64%

Copyright © 2023 - Ya Hala Canada Immigration Inc. - All rights reserved

Colombia	77%	65%	62%	Poland	83%	97%	90%
Croatia	78%	85%	77%	Russia	73%	74%	67%
Czech Republic	92%	95%	97%	Singapore	85%	94%	92%
Denmark	86%	99%	90%	South Africa	62%	59%	73%
Egypt	54%	52%	55%	South Korea	95%	97%	96%
Ethiopia	13%	22%	14%	Spain	95%	97%	96%
Finland	91%	100%	96%	Sri Lanka	45%	45%	52%
France	93%	98%	92%	Turkey	73%	66%	47%
Germany	90%	98%	96%	Taiwan	92%	93%	88%
Ghana	34%	18%	18%	Thailand	81%	83%	83%
Greece	85%	88%	75%	UAE	59%	57%	62%
Hong Kong	84%	90%	87%	Ukraine	65%	72%	76%
Hungary	77%	91%	82%	USA	84%	94%	89%
India	64%	48%	60%	Venezuela	45%	50%	57%
Indonesia	79%	71%	72%	Vietnam	49%	61%	70%

One of the key factors in determining eligibility for a study permit is that the applicant must be a genuine student who is seeking to study in Canada. This implies that they are planning to stay in Canada temporarily while they study, but have solid connections to their home country that would allow them to return after their studies and continue their career. Students who have no intention of returning to their home country are very likely to stay in Canada illegally after the expiry of their study permit. They are also likely to work illegally in Canada. Therefore, applicants must convince the immigration officials reviewing their application that they are genuinely interested in studying in Canada, and that they will comply with the conditions of their visa.

Each country has a unique economic, social, and political situation. In some countries, these circumstances motivate students to avoid returning, even if this means staying in Canada illegally. Consequently, a higher number of students from these countries are assessed as being at a high risk of not complying with the requirements of their study permit status. Also, if the economic prospects of a student in their home country are not solid, this raises questions about why they are investing in an expensive international education in Canada, and whether they would return to the uncertain economic situation in their country or whether

they would likely decide to stay in Canada and work illegally to recover the costs of their education.

Therefore, it is important for you to understand the approval rate in your country. If you are from a country with a low approval rate, then you should work harder to convince the immigration officer reviewing your application that you are a genuine student, that you can have a great career when you return to your home country, and that the investment in an international education in Canada is a logical choice for you.

What to do if your Study Permit Application is Refused?

Applicants that fail to demonstrate that they meet the eligibility requirements for a study permit will receive a refusal letter. Online applicants will receive the letter through their online portal. The letter will explain, at a high level, the reasons for the refusal. The letter will also invite the applicant to re-apply if they believe that they meet the eligibility criteria.

Therefore, applicants who receive a refusal are encouraged to understand the reasons for the refusal and to re-apply if they believe that they can demonstrate that these reasons do not apply to them.

The most common reasons for refusal are:

1. **Suitability for the program of studies.** This grounds for refusal is often seen for applicants who are either not qualified to pursue the program they have been admitted to or are overqualified. For example, an applicant intending to go into a completely different area of study than their background might face a refusal on these grounds if the officer reviewing the application is not convinced that the chosen program of study is logical given the applicant's background and career path. Similarly, an applicant with a master's or PhD degree applying to do a bachelor's degree in Canada may face a refusal for similar reasons. It is therefore critical for applicants to demonstrate that the program they intend to study is appropriate and to explain their background and professional experience.

2. **Insufficient means for financial support.** This is a straightforward one but not easy to address. Applicants are expected to demonstrate their ability to pay their tuition fees and cover their living expenses for at least the first year of the program. If they cannot demonstrate that they have access to sufficient funds, then a refusal is to be

expected. Also, applicants who will spend their entire life savings to pursue a study program may be looked upon suspiciously, especially if their job prospects and expected income after graduation do not justify the investment. Similarly, applicants who plan on taking on large loans to finance their education must demonstrate why this makes sense given their future career prospects. Applicants who rely on large gifts from relatives or friends or whose bank accounts show large and unexplained transfers may also risk refusal due to being unable to clearly demonstrate financial ability to support themselves during their studies in Canada. Gifts from relatives or other sponsors must be clearly explained in a letter of support. Why is this person willing to give you this amount of money to pursue your studies? Is it really a gift or will they expect to be paid back? Unexplained transfers of money into your account must also be explained. Where did the money come from? If you sold an asset or received a distribution from an investment, then you should include supporting documentation.

3. **Unable to demonstrate the intention to return to their home country.** A study permit allows temporary residence in Canada to attend a study program. Applicants must therefore demonstrate enough ties to their home country to clarify that they intend to return home after their studies. A student planning to spend their entire life savings or go into heavy debt to finance studies in Canada and who cannot recoup their investment when they return to work in their home country are at high risk of staying in Canada illegally. Also, students who have never traveled abroad lack a trustworthy travel history and are also regarded as being at a higher risk of overstaying their visa. Applicants must therefore demonstrate enough ties to their home country through professional, career, investment, property ownership, and family relationships.

GCMS Notes

The refusal letters issued by the IRCC are brief and are built using pre-written template language. They are not tailored specifically to each case, but rather include broad statements about the reasons for the refusal. This makes it difficult to really understand the reasoning behind

the refusal, which leaves many student applicants wondering how they can strengthen their application in the future.

One strategy for getting more detailed information about any application to the IRCC is to request the GCMS (Global Case Management System) notes. The GCMS is the name of the system that is used by the IRCC and the Canada Border Services Agency (CBSA) to process and track applications. It contains a detailed record of each application, including the original application package, correspondence letters to and from IRCC, notes from the officers reviewing the file, and other data to track the status of the application.

The GCMS notes can be requested by submitting a request under the Access to Information Act, which is a law that allows people to access information about themselves that is held by the federal government. Permanent Residents and Canadian Citizens can directly request information under the Act, while foreign nationals must use a representative to make a request on their behalf.

The Canadian government operates an "Access to Information and Privacy (ATIP) Online Request" service that allows submission of requests for information through an online system. There is a minimal cost associated with each request. The cost is $5 Canadian dollars at the time of this

writing. The system also allows you to receive either the original application package and documentation submitted to the IRCC, the officer's notes, or both. The data can be delivered by CD or more conveniently through email.

GCMS notes requests typically take around 30 days, although it can take longer during periods where there is a heavier load of requests being received. So it is important for you to plan your timeline accordingly to ensure that you are able to wait 1 - 2 months to receive the GCMS notes.

This is one of the reasons why it is advisable for students to apply for a study permit as early as possible. In case of an application refusal, having sufficient time before the start of your study program will allow you to carefully plan your re-application strategy to maximize your chances of success. To be successful in a second or even third application, you will likely need to provide more evidence to support your application. Obtaining and translating documents can take time. Also, if you want to view the GCMS notes, you will need to have sufficient time to receive the notes before you re-apply.

The GCMS notes are not mandatory for re-applying for a study permit after a refusal. The student may re-apply at any time when they feel they are ready. In cases where the reasons for a refusal are well known and

understood, it may not be necessary or worthwhile to wait for the GCMS notes. For example, if the reason for a refusal is lack of proof of financial support, and the applicant is able to submit evidence of additional financial resources such as additional bank accounts or support from parents, then the GCMS notes will likely not be very helpful.

Although the GCMS notes package that you will receive from the IRCC is quite large and could contain tens or hundreds of pages in a PDF file, most of the information is not very helpful to you as an applicant. Much of the information is a print-out of the data submitted in the application as it's stored in the computer system. There is a small section that records the notes written by the officer on the application. The notes are usually only one or two paragraphs, and they briefly describe where the application meets the eligibility requirements and where it doesn't.

When an applicant is unsure of the reasons behind a refusal, the officer's notes can provide important insights into their thinking and reasoning for refusing the application. This can help the applicant build a subsequent application that is strong and that specifically addresses the concerns raised by the officer in their refusal, leading to a much better chance of overcoming the refusal and getting an approval.

Figure 8: Edmonton Skyline [13]

Re-Application Strategy

As discussed in the previous section, if you receive a refusal letter from the IRCC regarding your study permit application, then you have the opportunity to re-apply if you believe that you meet the eligibility requirements for receiving a study permit. However, simply re-applying with the same information and documentation will likely lead to another refusal.

---

[13] **Source:** awmcphee, CC BY-SA 4.0 <https://creativecommons.org/licenses/by-sa/4.0>, via Wikimedia Commons
https://commons.wikimedia.org/wiki/File:Edmonton_Skyline_from_106_Street_Lookout_2019_crop.jpg

To overcome the refusal, you must consider the reasons cited in the refusal letter. You may also review the officer's notes on your application by requesting the GCMS notes, as discussed in the previous section. Read the reasoning very carefully and write down the key points. Make a list of the reasons why the officer considers that you don't meet the eligibility requirements.

Once you have a clear understanding of the reasons for the refusal, take each point in the list and write down what arguments you can make to respond, and what documents you can use to support your arguments.

For example, if one of the reasons for the refusal is that the study program you intend to pursue is not suitable for you given your previous education and career path, then you can respond by discussing your background and your future plans, and explain why the study program you selected is a great fit. You may consider including additional documentation about your previous studies and letters of recommendation or records of employment to support your arguments.

As another example, if the reason for refusal is a lack of means of financial support, then you must determine whether you have submitted enough evidence to show that you have the financial means to pay your tuition fees and living expenses. Consider whether there are additional

documents you can provide, or other sources of funding and support that you can add to your application.

Finally, if the reason for the refusal is that the officer is not convinced that you will return to your home country, then you can think about what information and documentation you can provide to prove your ties to your home country. You may add evidence of assets you own, investments you have, and professional, social and family ties. You can also add evidence of previous travel (if applicable) to prove that you are a trusted traveler and that you have not overstayed your visas in the past. You can also discuss your future plans in more detail to demonstrate that you have a solid path forward upon your return to your home country. It also helps for you to clearly state that you understand that a study permit and visa only allows you to stay in Canada temporarily while you study, and that you understand that you will have to leave Canada and return to your home country.

Organizing your subsequent application

Once you have collected a list of the reasons for refusal, and you have made notes of your arguments and documents that you will use to respond to each of the items on the list, then you are ready to build your new application. Much of the application package will remain the same as

with your previous application, including the application forms, passport copies, photos, and other parts of the application that are not impacted by the refusal. Identify the parts of the application that must be updated, and re-work those parts to support your response to the refusal. For example, perhaps you have to update your budget and financial support documentation.

Update your letter of explanation to address the refusal. Start your letter by indicating that this is a subsequent application, and that your previous application was refused. Provide the previous application number and UCI (Unique Client Identification) number. Clearly state that you have added new information and documentation, and that you believe that you meet the eligibility requirements for a study permit. Tell the officer that you have responded to each of the reasons cited for the refusal in this letter.

After this introductory section, take each item on the list of reasons for the refusal and make it into a section heading. Then add your arguments and mention the documentation that you are using to address that concern. Make sure you are clear and concise in your writing. Officers often do not have a lot of time to review each application, and so you want to quickly and clearly address each point. Your goal is to help the officer to find the information and documents they need to see in order

to approve your application. So the more you can organize your application package and documentation, the easier it will be for the officer to understand your application and approve it.

Using the new letter of explanation, the updated parts of the application, and the rest of the standard forms and information, build the required PDF documents according to the requirements of the IRCC, and prepare them to upload. Make sure you haven't missed any documents, and that you have clearly addressed each point mentioned in the refusal letter. Once completed, you will be ready to submit the re-application using the same steps you followed for submitting your original application.

Summary: Re-application Strategy

- Re-applying with the same information and documents will likely lead to another refusal
- Carefully consider the reasons for refusal
- Request the GCMS notes if you have time and need a deeper insight into the reasons for refusal
- Make a list of arguments and documents you can use to respond to each of the reasons for refusal
- Organize your re-application carefully to quickly address the reasons of refusal
- Start with a list of the reasons of refusal
- Write a section to address each of these reasons
- Don't let the stress of the situation cause you to rush the application and make mistakes
- Take your time!

Case Study 3 - Dealing with a Study Permit Refusal

Eduardo had received admission to Ivey business school at Western University, one of the top business schools in Canada. He could hardly contain his excitement! The application process was not easy. After submitting a full application package including an essay explaining why he would be a good fit for the school, he was asked to do an interview with the admissions team. He was confident and was able to clearly explain his background and his future career goals.

As soon as he was informed that he was accepted into the program, he immediately called his family and friends, and he went out for a special dinner to celebrate that night. His admission came with a generous scholarship, and the director of the program had written him a letter welcoming him. Within a few weeks, he began to make travel arrangements. He booked his flight and a hotel for his first week in Canada, and he started a list of all the things he wanted to take with him.

To his shock, his study permit application was refused. In the excitement of everything else going on, he had quickly logged into the online portal, and put together a quick application. How hard could it be? A few forms, a copy of his passport, and a copy of his bank statement. After all, he had already passed the hard part, which is getting admission to his dream program.

He read the refusal letter in total disbelief. All of his dreams flashed in front of his eyes, and he felt that all his plans were shattered. How embarrassing is it going to be to tell his parents and friends this news?

The refusal letter stated that he did not show that he had enough financial resources to cover the costs of his stay in Canada. It also said that the officer did not believe that he would leave Canada at the end of his stay.

How could this be? He had submitted his bank statements. His family has a very successful business, and his father who was the CEO had already offered him the position of VP of Marketing as soon as he came back home after graduation.

Eduardo thought all was lost. But he contacted an immigration consultant, just in case there was something that could be done. The consultant helped Eduardo to think through his application, and he realized that he had forgotten to attach proof that he had received a scholarship! He also was counting on some financial support from his parents, but he never included their bank statements or a letter of support. And in his application, he never mentioned his future plans or his job offer which he planned to take after graduation.

How could he have made such silly mistakes? Eduardo was so disappointed in himself. How would the immigration officer reviewing his application know that he had enough money or that he had a job waiting for him after graduation? He pulled himself together, and he worked closely with the immigration consultant for 2 weeks to build a better and stronger application. They reviewed it together multiple times, and brainstormed every possible argument and document they could provide.

A few weeks after submitting his second application, Eduardo got a request to send in his passport for visa stamping. His application had been approved! Eduardo's only regret was that he didn't invest enough time in his first application, as he could have avoided all this drama and

heartache. But regardless, he was super excited that his dreams were back on track, and that his plane tickets were not wasted!

STEP 4: Arriving in Canada

Travel and Arrival in Canada

If a study permit application is approved, the applicant will receive a letter through the online portal (if they applied online) requesting that their passport be submitted to the nearest visa application center (VAC). A temporary residence visa will be stamped into the passport (if required). For students from countries where a visa is not required, an eTA will be issued instead. Besides the visa or eTA, the applicant will also receive a letter of introduction. Upon entering Canada, this letter will show that a study permit has been approved. The study permit will then be issued to the student if the border services officers are satisfied that the student still meets the eligibility requirements.

While many students get excited about the prospect of studying in Canada and exploring a new country, it is highly recommended to wait until your study permit has been approved before booking confirmed travel tickets. Many travel bookings are non-refundable, and so the money spent to buy tickets will be lost if the study permit is refused. It is advisable to apply several months in advance of planned travel, keeping in mind the current processing times published by the IRCC, to allow enough time to book tickets and make travel arrangements.

Figure 9: Air Canada airplane at Vancouver International Airport [14]

---

[14] **Source:** Quintin Soloviev, CC BY-SA 4.0 <https://creativecommons.org/licenses/by-sa/4.0>, via Wikimedia Commons
https://commons.wikimedia.org/wiki/File:Air_Canada_-_Boeing_767-375ER_-_C-FOCA_(Quintin_Soloviev).jpg

Students are typically expected to arrive in Canada no more than 30 days before the official start date of their study program as per the official letter of acceptance from their institution. Students who arrive earlier than 30 days may have to return home and only come back to Canada within that time frame. Arriving too early before the start of your study program raises questions about whether your budget can accommodate a longer stay. It also raises questions about what you plan to do during this time, especially since you are not allowed to work. All these factors are taken into consideration by the border services officers at the airport who will make the final decision on permitting your entry to Canada and granting you a study permit.

Remember, the study permit and associated visa are issued to study in Canada. Therefore, arriving early to tour Canada or visit family and friends before starting the study program is not in line with the purpose of the visa. There will be plenty of time while you are in Canada during weekends, holidays, and study breaks to visit places, go sightseeing, and meet with family and friends.

What to Bring with you to Canada?

Once your travel is booked, you will pack your bags and think about what you need to bring with you to Canada. Most importantly, don't forget to bring all your original documentation related to your study permit application. Remember, your study permit is not issued until you arrive in Canada, and the border services officers at the airport may ask to see your documentation. So besides your passport, you will need to bring these documents:

1. Your letter of introduction.

2. Letter of acceptance from the educational institution.

3. Means of financial support documentation, including your budget and supporting documents such as bank statements, letters of support, loan letters, deposit and tuition fee payment receipts, and scholarship letters. If your original bank statements are outdated by the time you arrive in Canada, bring new statements so you can prove that the money is still available in your accounts.

4. Letter of Explanation and all supporting documents attached to it.

5. Your previous educational degrees, certificates, and transcripts/marksheets.

6. Any other documentation included in your application for the study permit or that would demonstrate your eligibility for a study permit.

Beyond the required documentation for your study permit, you are also advised to bring some cash and credit cards as needed to support yourself for the first few weeks while you arrange to open bank accounts and access your sources of funds. Government regulations may limit the amount of cash and equivalents you can carry with you, or they may require you to declare the amount you are carrying. Confirm this information before your travel to ensure that you comply with all regulations.

Also, don't forget to bring confirmation of hotel and transportation bookings or other similar arrangements you have made, including contact numbers you need. Having a working cell phone capable of making calls while roaming in Canada is helpful in your first few days while you get your Canadian cell phone number. You may want to get a global roaming sim card that would allow you to get service while traveling.

If you are arriving in the winter months, don't forget to pack warm clothes! Clothing that can be layered is advisable, as it can be used in different temperatures. Also, a heavy coat is necessary to brave Canadian winters, where temperatures are frequently below freezing. Warm winter boots, if available, or at least footwear with good traction to allow walking on ice and snow is highly recommended. You will likely want to purchase some of these items in Canada. But if you are arriving in the

winter, having a few winter outfits to get through your first couple of weeks is a good idea.

Summary: What to bring to Canada
<ul><li>Documents:<ul><li>Passport</li><li>Letter of introduction</li><li>Financial documents (originals)</li><li>Letter of explanation and all attachments</li><li>Degrees, certificates, and transcripts/marksheets</li><li>Hotel and transportation bookings</li></ul></li><li>Cash and/or credit cards that will work in Canada</li><li>Cell phone with ability to roam in Canada</li><li>Non-slippery shoes in case of snow/ice</li><li>Warm clothes</li></ul>

Accommodations

You have a number of options for accommodations in Canada. Your educational institution can likely help you with suitable options locally where you will be studying. Some colleges and universities will have "student residences" (also known as dorms). Student residences are very convenient because they are often on or close to the main campus, allowing you to easily access all university classes and facilities within

walking distance. This eliminates the need to buy a car or arrange other transportation. Student residences sometimes also offer a meal plan that allows you to eat at selected restaurants or cafeterias, which can relieve you from spending time and effort preparing and cooking food. However, student residences can be more expensive than other options. You may also have to share a room with a roommate, and in some residences, washroom facilities are shared among a number of students on the same floor. The rooms can also be rather small and are usually limited to a bed and a small desk.

Many students who want the flexibility of more options to choose their accommodation opt to live off-campus. Many campuses have nearby neighborhoods or buildings geared for student life, and these can range from rooms within a house, to shared apartments, or even your own independent apartment. This allows the student more control over how much they want to spend and the lifestyle they would be most comfortable with. Costs are often managed by sharing with a roommate to split the costs.

Most Canadian cities have decent public transportation networks and affordable student transportation passes that allow students to travel between their home and campus, and to other locations within the city conveniently and cost effectively. It is advised to think about

transportation options when choosing your accommodation to ensure that it will be convenient for you.

Some students choose to live in a university residence in their first year in Canada, for the simplicity and convenience. After the first year, they will have become familiar with the city they live in and may choose to move off campus to save costs or to enjoy more flexible living arrangements.

Once you are settled in your accommodation, you will have a mailing address. This is important as you can use it in government, banking, and telecommunications transactions. Also, a cell phone and a working cell phone number are necessary to facilitate many activities. Explore the available mobile phone providers as the prices and features can vary greatly. Most students choose one of the budget providers to get basic mobile phone coverage, at least initially. It is advisable to avoid signing long-term contracts early on and to select a provider that allows cancellation and moving of your service and phone number.

Internet access will also be necessary, and as with mobile phone providers, prices can vary widely. Do your research and select a provider that offers decent service without locking you into a long-term contract. Since you may need reliable internet access for your studies, it is important to have a relatively high-speed internet connection to allow for

video streaming and video conferencing as needed. Also, you may use your internet connection to communicate with your family and friends, so make sure the plan is unlimited or provides enough bandwidth to cover your expected activities.

Figure 10: Toronto Skyline [15]

---

[15] **Source:** Raysonho @ Open Grid Scheduler / Grid Engine, CC0, via Wikimedia Commons
https://commons.wikimedia.org/wiki/File:SkylineToronto2.jpg

Case Study 4 - At the airport in Canada!

Temitope had been waiting for this moment for months! After a long process and lots of effort, her plane was finally landing at Halifax Stanfield International Airport. Her Medical Laboratory Technology diploma program will be started in just 3 weeks! She was super excited to finally see the campus of the Nova Scotia Community College. She has been reading about it and looking at photos online for months, but today she was going to finally see it in real life!

It was not easy getting here. First, she spent months convincing her parents that studying in Canada was a good idea. They could not imagine her being away for 3 years! And what about her two younger brothers. The family needed Temitope. But she finally convinced them that studying in Canada would open a lot of doors for her.

Temitope's parents wanted what is best for her, of course. But finances were tight. They did not know how they would be able to afford her education. They had saved some money over the years, and it would be enough to pay her tuition fees for the first year. Luckily, Temitope was able to secure an educational loan that covered the rest of her expenses. This, along with doing some part-time work, would be enough to get her through the program. It wasn't going to be an easy or luxurious life, but she was willing to go through it for a better future.

Once her family was on board, and her financial plan was in place, Temitope spent many sleepless nights working on her study permit application. She knew that it would not be automatic, and that she would have to convince the officer that studying in Canada made sense.

She worked on a very well-written letter to accompany her application. She explained her background, her future dreams, how she would

finance her education, and also why studying in Canada made sense. She explained that upon returning to Nigeria, she would be able to work at one of the major hospitals, where pay would be very good. With a diploma from a great College in Canada, she would be sought after among employers, and they would even offer her a higher salary than if she had studied in Nigeria.

It worked! She got approval for her study permit, and now she was at the airport in Halifax. She proceeded to speak with the immigration officer. The officer asked to see her passport, and to explain the reason for her visit. Temitope was a bit nervous, but she had brought all the necessary paperwork with her.

She presented her passport, letter of introduction, and the college acceptance letter, and she told the officer that she is requesting a study permit. The officer asked her a few routine questions. How long is her program? Where would she be staying? And what is she bringing with her into Canada?

He then asked to see her financial plan to confirm that she still had enough finances to cover her costs. Temitope had been prepared. She took out updated bank statements, her parents letter of support, and her loan approval letter. After a quick inspection, the officer returned her documents and started typing on his computer.

A few minutes later, he printed Temitope's study permit, gave it to her, and said welcome to Canada! Temitope checked the study permit to confirm all the details were correct. Then, she smiled and said thank you as she walked past immigration and into Canada!

STEP 5: Studying in Canada

Studying in Canada

Key skills to develop

Educational institutions vary widely around the world in terms of their expectations of students, and how they assess a student's performance. So it is important for you to understand what will be expected of you before you start your studies in Canada. Some common skills will be needed for any program, such as good communication skills. Most educational programs and courses require some student participation and group work. So your ability to communicate with your classmates and express yourself comfortably in oral presentations and in writing is very important. Many educational institutions offer language training programs for incoming international students who require extra training before starting their chosen program of study.

Beyond having sufficient language skills, students are expected to be able to clearly express themselves orally and in writing. Strong communication skills are expected during participation in class, in assignments, tests, exams, and group work. Students will also typically be expected to present their work to their teacher and classmates. Incoming students are not necessarily expected to master all these skills from day 1 but will rather develop these skills during their studies.

Another important skill expected of students at Canadian post-secondary institutions is critical thinking, which is the ability to analyze issues and form an opinion on them. Critical thinking is characterized by deep thinking and questioning of all aspects of an issue to form a deeper understanding. This contrasts with simply believing the commonly accepted understanding of an issue, or re-stating information found in your study materials. Rather, a student is expected to determine advantages and disadvantages and to weigh the pros and cons, before making a judgment based on a deep analysis of the subject.

The ability to work both independently and in groups is also an important skill. Post-secondary students are expected to spend many hours independently reading and studying. Professors and course instructors at the post-secondary level will typically not have the time to explain all concepts. The classes serve as a way for the instructor to direct the students, summarize ideas, engage in discussions and group work, and highlight key areas to study. Students are then expected to spend time outside of the classroom to read textbooks and other references to ensure that they are gaining an understanding of the required concepts.

Group work is also an important part of most post-secondary studies in Canada. Students are expected to work with others on assignments, projects, and presentations. The group must learn to organize

themselves, manage their time, divide tasks between group members, and deal with conflicts or issues between team members. These teamwork skills are important to develop because they facilitate the transition to the workplace. So it is in your own best interest to take advantage of any opportunities to build your teamwork and leadership skills while you are still a student.

Post-secondary studies in Canada are demanding and the expectations are high. You are advised to dedicate yourself completely to your studies. Expect to focus completely on your studies, and not be involved in many social activities or long hours of work. Maintain your mental and physical health by exercising, spending time with friends, and having some entertainment. But you are expected to manage your time to ensure these activities do not interfere with your ability to complete your courses. If you work part-time while studying (if allowed under your study permit), this will be at the expense of something else in your life.

Course planning

Understand the specific prerequisites for any program you are interested in before applying. For example, many college diploma programs and university undergraduate programs require graduation from a secondary school. Some programs, such as engineering, expect you to have taken

certain courses during your secondary school education, such as Algebra, Calculus, or Physics. Make sure that you have the prerequisites for the program you are interested in, and if you don't, choose another program or enroll in the required courses to ensure that you will be eligible for admission.

Most universities and colleges have academic advisers that can help you with course planning and selection. They can guide you through understanding which courses you must take in order to be able to advance through your program. It is also important to think of your goals while choosing courses. Make sure that your course selections keep the doors open for you to reach your goals.

For example, if you are in an electrical engineering program and would like to specialize in electronics, make sure that you take the required courses each semester that will allow you to pursue your desired electronics courses. If you don't pay attention to this point, you may find that by the time you reach your fourth year, you are missing some basic courses that prevent you from taking the fourth year courses that you really want.

Academic expectations

It's also important to understand the difference between college, university undergraduate, and university graduate programs. College programs typically have easier entry requirements, so expectations may be more relaxed. Many students find it easier to achieve high grades in college courses compared to university programs. However, significant effort and dedication is required to succeed. Do not expect that you can simply pass your classes without putting in the required effort.

University undergraduate programs are often intense, with many courses in parallel and an expectation that you will be able to manage your time to complete required assignments and projects, and pass tests and exams. In a university program, there is less interaction with professors and it is easy to fall behind. If you are enrolled in a university program, you must work hard to stay with the class. Beyond attending lectures, you must put in many hours outside of class time to read textbooks, review notes, and complete assignments and projects. You will often have to go beyond the material taught in class to ensure that you solidly understand the material, and to fill in any gaps in your understanding.

Graduate university programs are either course-based or research-based. Course-based master's programs are somewhat like undergraduate

university programs in that you must complete a set number of courses to graduate. Some of these programs also require a major project or written paper at the end to secure graduation. Master's level courses are of course more advanced than undergraduate courses, and typically require even more independent work to understand the course material. Master's level courses, particularly in science and engineering, will also require a lot of hands-on laboratory work. Grades are typically concentrated in a few major assignments, projects, or exams.

Research-based graduate programs, including Master's and PhD degrees may require some coursework, but most of the effort in these programs is research-based. Students are often expected to contribute to research projects led by their supervising professor or a more senior member of their research group. They are also expected to carry out their own research and write a thesis to document their findings. While Master's level research can often be exploratory of existing research, PhD degrees typically require the student to perform original research and contribute something new to the field they are working in. The research supervisor will guide the student towards research that would fulfill the requirements to graduate.

Research-based Master's and PhD students will also be expected to "defend" their thesis in front of a panel of professors. The thesis defence

involves presenting the research and answering questions from the panel. If satisfied with the student's work, the panel will pass the student and allow them to graduate and receive their degree. The supervising professor plays a key role in guiding the student and ensuring that they are ready for the thesis defence.

Research-based graduate students are also typically expected to work at the university either as Teaching Assistants or Research Assistants. As a teaching assistant, the student is expected to support other students by holding office hours, correcting assignments, supervising lab work, or teaching classes. Research assistants are expected to support a research project and their work may include finding and summarizing research papers on certain topics, participating in research activities, and contributing to writing or reviewing research papers. Teaching and Research assistants are typically compensated for their work, which helps these students to cover their tuition and living expenses.

Cheating and Plagiarism

It cannot be emphasized enough that cheating and plagiarism are not tolerated at Canadian educational institutions. Cheating includes copying assignments from classmates, other friends or relatives, or from the internet. Cheating on tests and exams includes attempting to copy

answers from another student's paper or bringing in notes or other materials when you are instructed not to do so. It's important to understand and respect the rules of exams and assignments. Some tests may be "open book" which typically means that you may refer to certain materials during the test. But most test and exams allow only specific items, for example you may be allowed a calculator during a mathematics exam.

Plagiarism is copying other people's work directly and without attribution to the original author. Even copying a single sentence exactly as it is from another source and into your own work is considered plagiarism if you do not attribute this sentence to the original author. While explaining the rules of citing sources is beyond the scope of this book, know that plagiarism can result in serious consequences. This can range from a refusal to mark your work, getting a zero on that piece of work and in severe cases, could result in expulsion from the study program.

The use of artificial intelligence tools to automatically generate text that you present as your own original work is also a form of plagiarism. Although you may of course use research tools, research engines, and artificial intelligence software to collect information and to help you understand certain concepts, any work you submit to the university or college must be original.

Beyond the consequences of cheating and plagiarism, you must remember that you have spent a significant amount of money and dedicated a portion of your life to getting your diploma or degree. This is your opportunity to learn. So take advantage of this opportunity and put in the effort to learn and do your work independently. While you may be able to get wonderful marks by cheating or copying the work of others, you will graduate with very little knowledge or experience in doing work. This will negatively affect you for the rest of your career. So it's not worth it. Manage your time, focus on your studies, and put in the effort, and you will get great results!

Working While You Study

If allowed by your study permit, you may work part-time during your studies in Canada. You must have authorization in your study permit that explicitly allows you to work, and this may limit you to working "on-campus" and/or "off-campus". Working on campus typically involves being a teaching assistant, course instructor, or research assistant. Other various jobs on campus may be available, and most universities post these jobs online or on job boards on campus. Before you start working, you must check the most recent IRCC regulations regarding work without a work permit to ensure that you are in compliance. If you work when you are not authorized to do so, you are breaking the conditions of your

stay in Canada and this may result in you losing your status in Canada. Breaking the conditions of your study permit can also impact all future applications for temporary and permanent residence in Canada.

Off-campus work may also be allowed on your study permit if you meet certain conditions. This will typically allow you to work up to 20 hours per week during study semesters, and full-time during scheduled breaks in your study program such as winter or summer holidays. It is your responsibility to ensure that you meet the conditions and that you are eligible to work to avoid losing your status in Canada.

If you are eligible and interested in working, you must first obtain a Social Insurance Number (SIN). The SIN is a 9-digit number that the Government of Canada gives you, and you will need one to be able to work in Canada.

Although students should dedicate themselves to their studies and focus completely on studying, the ability to work while studying allows students to get income to help offset the costs of studying in Canada. If you work while studying, put in a clear plan to manage your time so you can meet all the requirements of your study program. It will not be easy to balance work and studying, so take it seriously and put in the effort to stay on track with your education.

Case Study 5 - Keeping up with a university program!

Amgad was always a top student. He came from a family that really cared about education. His father was a well known doctor in Egypt, and his mother was a professor at Cairo University. They raised their four kids to care deeply about education, to work hard, and to always excel academically. Amgad was the youngest child. His three sisters had all attended local universities and had already graduated with top honours. They were all working in great jobs now.

He had great role models to follow. And he had done really well throughout his schooling. In high school, he got the highest overall grade among his entire graduating class. Amgad was smart and sometimes he didn't even need to study for tests. He could also memorize quickly, and he remembered everything the teacher said in class. He could also read the textbooks quickly and be able to re-write the information in tests, so he always got top marks!

Just like they supported his sisters' education, Amgad's parents wanted to fully support him. They told him money was not an issue, as long as he got into a great program and did well. Amgad applied to universities in the UK and in Canada. After considering all his options, he chose the University of British Columbia (UBC). Vancouver looked like a beautiful city. And UBC was highly ranked globally.

Amgad got his study permit in May, because he didn't want to be rushed. He enjoyed his last summer in Egypt with his friends and family, and arrived in Vancouver in August to get settled into the university residence before his engineering program started in September.

The engineering program required students to take 6 courses in the first semester. The courses were Algebra, Calculus, Chemistry, Physics,

Computing Systems, and Mechanics. Amgad was used to keeping up with a lot of courses. But he still felt a bit nervous. Especially that now he was away from his family and in a new country. He had to make his own food and take care of his own laundry.

Amgad noticed another difference in his courses compared to all of his previous studies. Many of the courses required laboratory and project work, where he had to work with a team of students. It was not enough to just memorize what the textbook said. Amgad had to understand the concepts deeply enough and to put them into practice. He also had to do a lot of presentations to the professors in front of the entire class.

He also noticed that all the students around him were very bright. After all, admissions into UBC are highly competitive, so the students who were accepted were all at the top of their classes. Amgad was always used to standing out among his classmates, but in this program it would be more challenging to stand out.

The reality check came after the midterm exams. Amgad was shocked that he only got 62% on his Chemistry midterm. The lowest mark of his life! His other grades were not that impressive either. Amgad realized that he could not just continue as he had in the past.

He quickly learned that he had to work very hard to keep up with his courses. He spent all his free time between classes in the library, the study rooms, or the labs. He also needed to study on evenings and weekends, although he did not forget to have fun sometimes, enjoy the outdoors, and watch a movie once a month.

By the time of final exams, Amgad had been able to catch up and was much more confident. He achieved good grades and was on his way to success!

STEP 6: After You Graduate

After you Graduate

It's time to celebrate! You have completed all your program requirements and passed all your courses. Many universities will generate a letter indicating your successful completion of the program requirements. Once you receive this letter, it's time to think about your next steps.

Remember, when you entered Canada as a student, you were admitted as a temporary resident. This means that your stay in Canada is temporary, and you may stay only until your study program is complete. It is your responsibility to ensure that you maintain valid status in Canada at all times, and to never overstay your visa in Canada. Staying in Canada without a valid status can lead to you being asked to leave Canada and can have consequences if you ever want to visit Canada in the future.

There are several options you can choose from after you graduate:

1) Leave Canada to return to your home country
2) Extend your stay in Canada - as a student or tourist
3) Apply to stay in Canada to work (if eligible)

Before we discuss these options in a little bit more detail, let's talk about your study permit expiry.

Study Permit Expiry

Typically, your study permit expires on whichever date comes first:

- the date marked on the permit; or
- 90 days after the day you complete your studies

It is your responsibility to ensure that you always have a valid status in Canada. Upon expiry of your study permit, you will no longer have legal status in Canada. If you stay in Canada with an expired status, this can create issues for you in the future when applying for a visa or status in Canada. Therefore, you need to be always mindful of your valid status in Canada.

Sometimes, you may complete your studies before the expiry date marked on the study permit. In this case, your study permit expires 90 days after the date you complete your studies, even if this precedes the expiry date on the study permit. The 90 day period starts when you are notified by your school that you have completed the program, or when you receive your degree, diploma or certificate. The IRCC may confirm the date with the school to determine the expiry date of your study permit.

Sometimes, your study permit expiry date may be before you complete your studies. In such a situation, you must apply for an extension of your study permit. You must apply to extend your study permit at least 30 days

before your current study permit expires. If you apply before your permit expires, you can continue to study under the same conditions as your current study permit until the IRCC decides on your application to extend your study permit. However, you must remain in Canada while your extension application is being processed.

If your study permit expires while you are still studying in Canada, there is a process to restore your status as a temporary resident. Remember, you should never intentionally allow this to happen. However, sometimes students may forget or make a mistake. In this situation, you must apply to restore your status as a temporary resident in Canada, and apply for a new study permit. Under these circumstances, you may stay in Canada while your application is being processed. However, you may not resume your studies until you receive your new study permit.

Returning to your home country

Many students are eager to return to their home country upon completing their studies. Some students are sponsored through government programs or their employer and are expected to return to their home country upon completion of their studies. Other students are looking forward to employment opportunities and re-establishing

themselves back home. Perhaps most importantly, students are eager to reunite with their families and friends.

Figure 11: Maple Leaf [16]

As discussed in the previous section, be aware of the study permit expiration date to ensure that your travel plans take this into account. Plan to leave Canada before your study permit expires. Although you

---

[16] **Source:** Ktsquare from Canada, Public domain, via Wikimedia Commons
https://commons.wikimedia.org/wiki/File:Canadian_Maple_Leaf.JPG

might not realize it, at this point, you may have spent years in Canada, and you have probably accumulated a lot of stuff. Also, you've probably made friends whom you will want to see before you travel.

Therefore, it's important to prepare yourself and plan your trip home as early as possible. Ensure your rental agreement for your accommodations will expire and give notice as required. Write down a list of all your things, including clothes, electronics, books, kitchen utensils, sports equipment, and maybe even a car if you bought one. Decide which items you will take with you, and which items you want to sell, donate, or give away to your friends.

Remember that shipping items is expensive, so understand the cost of taking things with you on the plane or shipping them separately to decide what will work best for you. Give yourself enough time to sell used items through classified advertisements on campus, in your building, or online. Used clothing can be donated through local charities or at clothing donation bins which are available in most cities.

Don't forget to make your travel bookings and take care of all travel arrangements well ahead of your trip to avoid surprises. Read the latest travel advisories to make sure you understand any special travel requirements and make sure you are prepared.

Exchange contact information with friends in Canada so you can keep in touch. Also, many students like to take souvenirs and gifts from Canada for themselves and their family members back home, so set aside some time for any last-minute shopping you need to do before you travel.

Keep copies of your degree and transcripts, study permit, visa, and any other official documentation you received while in Canada. These may be helpful in the future if you ever decide to apply for another visa to Canada.

Extending your Stay in Canada

You can apply to extend your stay in Canada after your graduation. Remember, your study permit expires on the date marked on the permit or 90 days after the day you complete your studies, whichever comes first. Don't let your status in Canada expire. If you intend to stay in Canada, you must ensure that you maintain a valid status that allows you to legally stay in Canada.

Stay in Canada for Further Studies

Some students decide to pursue further studies in Canada after completing their first degree. For example, after completing an undergraduate degree, some students will pursue a master's degree. Or, after completing a master's degree, some students will continue their

graduate studies towards a PhD degree. College students may decide to pursue a second certificate or diploma after graduation. In such cases, you must apply to extend your study permit.

The process is like an application for a study permit from outside Canada, except that you can do it from inside Canada. You will need proof that you are continuing to study, such as a new letter of acceptance from your educational institution and proof of means of financial support, among other requirements. It is highly recommended that you apply for an extension of your study permit more than 30 days before the expiry of your current study permit. If you have applied for an extension, then you can stay in Canada and continue studying even if your study permit expires while you are waiting for a decision on your extension application.

If you plan on leaving Canada temporarily and then re-entering the country, make sure that you have a valid visa or Electronic Travel Authorization (eTA), depending on your country of citizenship. The only exception to this are US citizens, because they do not need a visa or eTA to travel to Canada. Check the expiry date on your visa/eTA and apply for a new one if needed. Having a valid study permit alone does not allow you to re-enter Canada, with limited exceptions.

Stay in Canada as a Visitor

If you would like to stay in Canada beyond the expiry of your study permit, but you are not planning to study or work, you can apply for a visitor record. For example, you may want to stay to attend your graduation ceremony, or to spend some time travelling in Canada as a tourist. Or perhaps your spouse or common-law partner has a valid study or work permit, and you want to stay with them in Canada. In these cases, you must apply for a visitor record, which gives you status as a visitor in Canada. The visitor record will have an expiry date, and this is the date you must leave Canada before. Once again, apply at least 30 days before the expiry of your study permit.

It is important to note that a visitor record is not a visa or eTA. This means that if you travel outside of Canada, you will need a visa or eTA (depending on your country of citizenship) to re-enter Canada. If your visa has expired, you will need to apply for a new visa if you are planning to leave Canada and re-enter. The visitor record alone will not permit you to enter Canada again.

Another important implication of extending your stay as a visitor is that once your study permit expires and you become a visitor, you are no longer eligible to apply for a study permit or work permit from within

Canada. This means you must leave Canada and apply from outside if you pursue further studies. So if you choose this option, make sure you understand the implications, and that extending your stay as a visitor will not give you more time to apply for an extension as a student/worker from within Canada. If you plan to continue your studies in Canada, then you need to plan to get all your documents ready so you can extend your study permit at least 30 days before it expires.

Stay in Canada as a Worker

Some students can secure a job in Canada before they graduate. It is possible to extend your stay in Canada as a worker. Students who graduate from a DLI program of at least 8 months and that leads to a certificate or a degree are eligible for a Post-Graduate Work Permit (PGWP). The PGWP is an open work permit that allows the holder to work for any employer anywhere in Canada. We will discuss the PGWP in the following section in more detail.

Sometimes, students who are not eligible for a PGWP may still apply for an extension of their stay in Canada as a worker. However, to receive a work permit for a foreign national, the employer may need to apply for a Labour Market Impact Assessment (LMIA), which is a document from Employment and Social Development Canada that says the employer is

allowed to hire a foreign national. There are exemptions from this process, but these complex scenarios are beyond the scope of this book.

Post-Graduate Work Permit (PGWP)

A post-graduate work permit (PGWP) allows eligible students to temporarily stay in Canada to work after graduation. This is a great opportunity offered to international students in Canada, as it allows them to gain some Canadian professional work experience before they return to their home country.

The PGWP is also very special because it is an "open work permit", which allows you to work in any occupation anywhere in Canada and change employers any time you wish (as long as the employer is not on the ineligible employers list). This is in contrast with most work permits that are restricted to a specific occupation or a specific employer.

Another great advantage of gaining Canadian work experience under a PGWP is that this work experience can improve your eligibility for permanent residence in Canada. Canada's permanent residency programs generally award applicants with points based on their age, education, language ability and work experience. Canadian work experience can increase your score, which improves your chances at being selected for permanent residency. Canadian work experience can also open up special

immigration programs reserved for those with Canadian experience, such as the Canada Experience Class (CEC) and some Provincial Nomination Programs (PNP).

Eligibility for a PGWP

To be eligible for a PGWP, you must have completed a study program at a designated learning institution (DLI) that was at least 8 months long and that led to a degree, diploma or certificate. You must also have maintained full-time status as a student in Canada during each semester of your study program, except for your last semester which can be part-time. Also, approved leaves of absence are allowed.

You must apply for a PGWP within 180 days after completing your program. If your study permit expired over 180 days before you apply, you are no longer eligible. A PGWP is also only available to you once in your lifetime. So if you graduated from a bachelor's degree program and got a PGWP afterwards, you cannot get another PGWP later if you study a master's program, since you have already used a PGWP once before. There are also other restrictions and exceptions beyond the scope of this book.

If your program is less than 8 months long, you are not eligible for a PGWP. If your program is over 8 months long and up to 2 years, the PGWP

will be valid for an equal length of time. For example, if your program was 18 months long, you are eligible for an 18-month-long PGWP. For programs longer than 2 years, a 3-year PGWP may be issued.

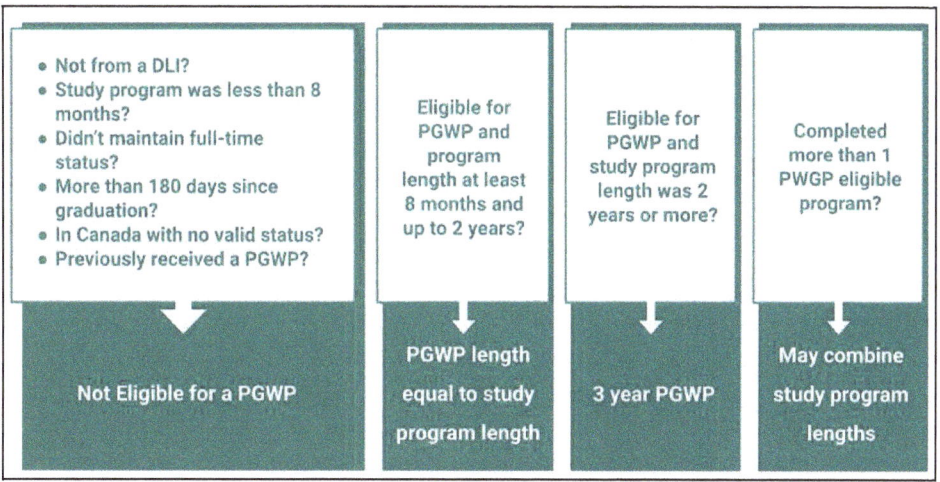

Figure 12: Post-Graduate Work Permit (PGWP) Scenarios

Students who complete more than one program of study may combine the length of the programs and qualify for a longer PGWP, if both programs are PGWP-eligible and at least 8 months in length. For example, if you completed an eligible 1-year certificate program, then you decided to study another 1-year certificate program, you may be eligible for a 2 year PGWP. Remember that you can only get one PGWP in your lifetime. So if you used your PGWP after your first 1 year certificate program and

worked for a year, you won't be able to get another PGWP even if you go back and study another PGWP-eligible program.

Make sure your passport is valid for the entire length of your PGWP. If your passport expires before the full length of your PGWP, it will only be issued with a validity period up to the expiry of your passport. You may extend it to the full length once you have renewed your passport. If you are eligible to extend your PGWP, this is typically noted on your initial PGWP.

Applying for a PGWP

If you are eligible for a PGWP, you must apply within 180 days after completing your study program. The application process is typically completed online for most students. You will need to prove that you've completed your studies in Canada by showing either a degree or diploma, an official letter from your school, and/or an official transcript. As with any application, additional documents may be required or requested by the IRCC.

The main application form required to apply for a PGWP is the "Application to Change conditions, Extend my Stay or Remain in Canada as a Worker (IMM 5710)". Supporting documents are also required,

including copies of your study permit and passport, and potentially other documents depending on your specific circumstances.

It is also recommended to include a cover letter explaining the reasons for your application for a PGWP. This is often attached to the application under the category of "Client Information", "Letter of Explanation", or "Additional Information", depending on the application portal you are using. While not required, it is highly recommended to ensure that all the facts and details surrounding your application are clear to the immigration officer. Also, it allows you to explain any issues or unusual things in your application.

You may use the cover letter to explain your background, where you are from when you entered Canada as a student, the program you completed, and why you are applying for a PGWP. You can also explain the length of the program, and details of your enrollment to ensure that you meet the eligibility requirements (for example, that you were enrolled full-time). You can use this letter to explain any leaves of absence or other special circumstances. This letter also allows you to add supporting documentation to your application, including evidence as to the length of your study program, to support your case for getting the appropriate PGWP length that you are eligible for.

Spouses and common-law partners of PGWP holders are also eligible to apply for an open work permit. Proof that the PGWP worker is employed in an occupation in skill type 0 or skill level A or B is required, such as a letter from the employer or a copy of the offer/contract, and a copy of the last 3 pay slips. This means that often your spouse or common-law partner must wait until the PGWP holder has 3 pay slips to be able to apply for an open work permit. If your spouse or common-law partner had received an open work permit while you were on a study permit and it is still valid, they may continue working according to the conditions of your work permit, and later extend it once you have evidence of your employment. Otherwise, if they didn't have an open work permit or if it has expired, they may need to stop working until they are issued a new work permit.

Maintained / Implied Status

PGWP applications may take several weeks to be processed. Luckily, students who apply for a PGWP before expiry of their study permit are considered to have "maintained status" (previously known as "implied status"). This means that you can start working immediately after you submit your PGWP application, under the same conditions as if you had an approved PGWP. Once you receive a positive result from your application, you can continue to adhere to the conditions of the PGWP. If

your PGWP is not approved, you must stop working immediately and leave Canada if you no longer have a valid status in Canada.

Figure 13: Domaine de Maizerets, Québec City [17]

---

[17] **Source:** Wilfredo Rafael Rodriguez Hernandez, CC0, via Wikimedia Commons
https://commons.wikimedia.org/wiki/File:Domaine_de_Maizerets,_Qu%C3%A9bec,_Canada.jpg

The Path to Permanent Residency

Many international students decide to stay in Canada permanently after graduation. Canada has generally welcomed and encouraged immigration since its founding in 1867. Immigration to Canada has supported economic growth and continues to be a priority for successive Canadian governments. Many of the immigration programs to Canada are focused on bringing skilled workers and workers with experience in specific occupations that are highly in demand in Canada. Most immigration programs require certain levels of education, work experience, and language skills.

International students who have graduated from Canadian universities are usually an excellent fit for Canada's immigration policy. They are already familiar with life in Canada and have received the same quality of education as Canadian graduates, which makes them well suited to find employment in Canada. Also, living in Canada for a number of years helps international students to develop their English and/or French language skills, which makes them highly likely to become successfully integrated into Canada's economy.

Figure 14: Ferry Terminal, Prince Rupert, British Columbia [18]

Most international students who graduate with a diploma or degree from a recognized Canadian educational institution will find several paths to permanent residency available to them. The Federal Skilled Worker Program (FWSP) is a great choice for many students. Applications for the FSWP are accepted through Canada's Express Entry (EE) system, where

---

[18] **Source:** Extemporalist, CC0, via Wikimedia Commons
https://commons.wikimedia.org/wiki/File:MV_Northern_Adventure_at_the_Prince_Rupert_Ferry_Terminal.jpg

foreign nationals can create a profile to express their interest in immigrating to Canada. A point system awards each candidate a number of points based on the Comprehensive Ranking System (CRS). The CRS score awarded to each candidate is based on their age, level of education, English and/or French language proficiency, and work experience. A detailed breakdown of the CRS points system is provided in Appendix B for your convenience, although you are encouraged to refer to the most updated information on the IRCC web site.

Once a candidate's profile is completed and a CRS score is awarded, the profile remains active in the express entry pool of candidates for 12 months. Rounds of invitations for permanent residency are held regularly, where a minimum cutoff score is used to identify the top-scoring candidates in the pool. Those with CRS scores above the cutoff are invited to apply for permanent residency, which allows these candidates to submit a full permanent residency application.

In 2023, Canada introduced a new category-based selection process for Express Entry. This process enables Canada to invite candidates who meet certain criteria, such as French language proficiency, work experience in a specific occupation, or education in a certain field or at a certain level. Regardless of the selection process, candidates who meet the minimum criteria are invited to submit a full permanent residency application.

Besides proving the education, language proficiency, and work experience as per their express entry profile, candidates must also submit police certificates and undergo a medical examination. If the candidate is found eligible for Canadian Permanent Residency (PR), they will be sent a visa and a Confirmation of PR (CoPR) document that they can use to obtain their PR status.

The FSWP is perhaps the most common path for international students towards permanent residency in Canada. For international students, having graduated from a Canadian institution and having spent time in Canada often translates into higher education, work experience and language proficiency scores, and increased the chances of receiving an invitation to apply for PR.

Canadian work experience gained under a Post-Graduate Work Permit (PGWP) can also boost a candidate's score. Having at least 12 months of Canadian work experience awards a candidate points for having Canadian work experience. It also opens the door to eligibility under the Canada Experience Class (CEC). This increases the chances of receiving an invitation to apply for permanent residency because these candidates can receive invitations from both the FSWP and CEC streams.

Beyond the FSWP and the CEC, many provincial immigration programs are tailored for students who graduate from the province or have work experience or a job offer from an employer in that province. Some provincial immigration programs select candidates from the Express Entry pool of candidates, and having Canadian education and work experience can be a factor in the selection process. These Provincial Nomination Programs (PNP's) provide yet another path to permanent residency in Canada.

Although there are no guarantees that an international student will eventually be successful in obtaining Canadian permanent residency (PR), most students who pursue this path are eventually successful through one of the many pathways to permanent residency. After living in Canada for 3 years, permanent residents may be eligible to apply for full Canadian citizenship. There are some eligibility criteria, including filing tax returns, proving language proficiency, passing a citizenship test, and taking the oath of citizenship.

Case Study 6 - From student to permanent resident

Darsh lived in the bustling capital of India, New Delhi. He was a recent BBA graduate, who was always on the search for opportunities that would change his life. A voracious reader, he spent hours exploring the advantages and perks of living abroad: top-notch healthcare, potential for massive earnings, comprehensive facilities, a stress-free lifestyle, happiness, and exposure to diverse cultures.

The idea germinated in his mind, and he finally concluded that Canada was the place to be for his higher education. With a plethora of opportunities abroad, Darsh was sure that an MBA from Canada would settle his life just the way he dreamed.

He approached his father to discuss his plans, not sure how the conversation would unfold. To his surprise, his father was supportive and agreed to manage the financial aspects of studying abroad. Both father and son realized that the initial investment would be substantial but worth it in the long run.

Darsh spent many hours researching and filling out university applications, and he was thrilled to finally receive his acceptance letter from Dalhousie University in Halifax. He put in a lot of effort to obtain his study permit, and eventually arrived in Canada for his MBA program. His dedication and tireless work paid off when he graduated at the top of his class.

But Darsh had much bigger dreams. He applied for a post-graduate work permit (PGWP), and received a 3 year open work permit. He landed a job with a large management consulting firm and started working diligently. Darsh was living the dream he had envisioned; life was comfortable and fulfilling.

After more than 2 years in Canada, Darsh was getting used to life here. He had a circle of friends, and they had a lot of fun together. In the winters, he learned to Ski. He also enjoyed skating, although it was quite hard to master, and he fell down a lot. In the summers, he explored hiking in the many parks and nature reserves. He also started following hockey, and really enjoyed watching games with his friends.

Most importantly, he met a wonderful woman during a project he was working on. Angela was incredibly smart and successful, and he really enjoyed spending time with her. He started to dream about building a life together with her. He really felt that Canada was becoming home.

Darsh researched the express entry programs available to him. With his Master's degree and Canadian work experience, he knew he would be eligible to apply for permanent residency (PR). He created an express entry profile, and within a couple of months he was invited to apply for PR. He carefully collected all the required documentation, and submitted a full and complete application.

Six months later, Darsh was a landed immigrant and permanent resident of Canada! He could now start planning for life in Canada for the long term. The first thing he did was to propose to Angela, and she said yes! They started planning their wedding, and they collected their savings for a downpayment on a small home.

Reflecting on his journey, Darsh realized that the life he was living now was beyond what he had initially dreamed of. He was enjoying all the benefits of being a Canadian permanent resident, had a great job, owned a home, and was starting a family. He was also contributing positively to his new society by paying taxes, donating to charities, and volunteering for good causes. Dreams sometimes do come true!

STEP 7: Hire Professional Help

Get Professional Help with your Visa and Immigration Needs

After reading this book, you probably realize that there is a lot more complexity to student visa and immigration applications than you could have possibly imagined. And you are right! Although we have tried our best to give you an overview of the process and requirements in this book, there is a lot more complexity involved than we could possibly cover. The rules and policies often vary depending on the country of the applicant. Also, the policies are constantly changing, making it difficult to stay updated with the latest and most accurate information.

Besides all that, each applicant's situation is unique. Some applicants are single, others are married or are in common-law relationships. Some have children, others do not. Some applicants have extensive travel histories, while others have never been outside of their own country. Some are applying from their home country where they are well established, while others have been living as expats for many years. Some applicants have the funds required to pay for their tuition and living expenses in the bank, while others require loans or family support. Each situation requires careful consideration and planning to determine the best strategy for your application. Professional immigration lawyers or Regulated Canadian Immigration Consultants (RCIC's) have experience dealing with these

scenarios and can provide invaluable advice to help you maximize the chance of getting approval.

But Internet Discussion Boards are Full of Immigration Advice!

Internet discussion boards or forums are full of people sharing their experiences with immigration and visa applications to Canada, as well as questions and answers about visa applications, immigration policies, how to complete forms, and many other topics.

There are two major problems with using these as sources of information. The first problem is that the people asking the questions and more importantly those giving the answers are anonymous. Nobody knows who they are or if they truly have accurate information about immigration matters. Also, those sharing their experiences rarely provide full personal details to allow you to understand the context well enough to judge whether their experience would apply in your situation or not.

The second major problem is that much of the information found with online searches is many years out of date. Keep an eye on the date of the post you are reading, and you will often find that you are reading information from 10 or 15 years ago, or more! Even reading information from last year is risky, let alone decades-old information!

Therefore, you are highly advised to avoid referring to or using information from such unverified sources while building and submitting your visa or immigration application.

Applying Independently Without Professional Help

If you decide not to hire a professional to help you with your visa application, make sure to follow the official guides and information provided by the IRCC. All the information you need is available, and the IRCC has made it possible for you to apply independently without hiring a representative or getting professional advice.

For study permits, the IRCC pages related to studying in Canada provide excellent context about eligibility requirements, how to apply, and what to expect. The IRCC also provides application guides that help you complete the required forms for each application. If you follow these instructions, you should be able to successfully complete the process independently.

Applying by yourself without professional assistance simply requires you to invest more effort and time to go through and understand the requirements on your own, and to follow the guides to ensure that you complete the application appropriately. Therefore, if you can read and

understand detailed instructions and follow them carefully, then you should find all the information you need.

Nonetheless, we do believe that hiring professional help can not only relieve you of the stress and anxiety of going through the process alone, but it can also increase your chances of success. A professional will have seen many applications before and will be familiar with common areas that result in a visa refusal if not appropriately handled.

Remember that having a visa refusal on your record can make all future visa applications to Canada more difficult. So don't take the possibility of a visa refusal lightly. Rather, make sure you take all precautions to minimize the chance of getting a refusal. Hiring a professional to guide you or at least review your application before submission is therefore highly advisable.

So don't wait until you have received a refusal to seek professional help! The time to seek professional help is before you submit your application.

Immigration Fraud and Unlicensed Immigration Consultants

Canadian immigration fraud is unfortunately very common. If you hire professional help to support you with your visa or immigration application, make sure that you are dealing with a licensed Canadian immigration consultant. Only lawyers registered in one of Canada's 13

Law Societies, notaires registered with the Chambre des notaires du Québec, and Regulated Canadian Immigration Consultants (RCIC's) are permitted by Canadian law to give immigration consultations.

Unlicensed immigration consultants can seriously and permanently damage your chances of receiving a visa or immigrating to Canada. This is because they are not trained on Canadian immigration law, and they are not accountable to anyone for their professionalism and ethics.

Most unlicensed immigration consultants will use any means possible, regardless of whether it is legal or not. They will often advise applicants to lie on their application, or fabricate documents, or hide information. These tactics may sometimes be successful, but they will very likely be discovered and result in very serious consequences for you. For example, if you are found to have misrepresented yourself in your application, by hiding information or providing false or inaccurate information, you can be banned from entering Canada for at least 5 years. You will also have a permanent record of fraud in your file with the Canadian government. If you already entered Canada, you could be charged with a crime or removed from Canada, and you could lose your status as a permanent resident. The unlicensed immigration consultant will have lost one client out of thousands, but your life will be impacted severely for a long time.

Ya Hala Canada Immigration Inc.

Ya Hala Canada Immigration Inc. was established in 2018, and has since worked with hundreds of clients. We specialize in study permits and have helped hundreds of students get their study permits. We have also worked with many students who initially received a refusal on their study permit application, and we have a good track record of helping them to get approvals on their second study permit application attempt.

Beyond study permits, we also work with clients on post-graduate work permits (PGWP), spousal open work permits, visitor visas, and permanent residency applications. What distinguishes our team is not just our deep experience and successful track record, but we also pride ourselves on providing quality service. This is why most of our business comes through word-of-mouth referrals from past clients.

It would be our pleasure to work with you on your study permit application, or any other Canadian visa or immigration matter. Please contact our team to get started!

Case Study 7 - Working with an immigration consultant

Aisha was super excited when she received her admission to the Animation program at Algonquin College! She loved art and drawing ever since she was a child, and dreamed of a career in an animation studio where she would have the opportunity to express her creativity. Aisha had also read a lot about Ottawa, and was excited that she would live in Canada's capital city for 3 years.

As her excitement continued to build, Aisha was determined not to make any mistakes with her study permit application. So she decided that she needed help from a professional. She had seen an advertisement in the local paper from a company that prepares visa applications for Canada. So she called them, and soon started the process of sharing documentation with them.

Within a couple of weeks, her study permit application was submitted! Best of all, the person who helped her with the application only took 20% of their fees upfront, and would only get paid the rest of the amount if Aisha received her study permit. So Aisha felt quite confident that it was only a matter of time before she would get her visa and study permit, and she would be on her way to Canada!

Aisha was shocked a few weeks later when she received news that her study permit application was refused. The officer had determined that she was not eligible for a visa because she didn't demonstrate that she had sufficient financial resources to cover her costs in Canada. The officer also noted that Aisha hadn't demonstrated that her intention was to stay in Canada temporarily.

In a bit of a panic, Aisha called the office that had submitted her visa application. No one was available to answer, so she left a message.

When no one got back to her by the next day, she left another message, and then another one. A few days later, someone finally answered. When Aisha asked for details on what happened, she was told that some applications get refused and there is nothing they can do. But the good news is that she would not have to pay the rest of the fees, because her application was refused.

Aisha was devastated. She didn't care about saving a few hundred dollars, when her entire dream of joining one of the best animation programs in Canada was evaporating in front of her eyes. She started yelling, but the person could only say sorry and then hung up.

Feeling like she was out of options, Aisha went online and searched the name of the office that had helped her with the application. She discovered hundreds of complaints from people like her. She also found out that this was an unofficial and unregistered consultant. They were not recognized by the Canadian government and in fact they were breaking the law by offering immigration consultations without a license.

She was shocked to learn all of this information. She felt cheated and betrayed. But she didn't understand why they only took 20% of the fee upfront? After reading more reviews online, she discovered that the way this company operated was that they submitted hundreds of visa applications with minimal effort. They didn't really care if the application got approved or refused. They just played a numbers game by submitting so many applications. And when some applications got approved, they would get a big bonus payment! For them, their focus was on collecting as many customers as possible and submitting as many applications as possible. The quality of the applications or whether they got approved or not was not important.

Aisha did not know that legitimate Canadian immigration consultants must be licensed by the College of Immigration and Citizenship Consultants (CICC). She also didn't know that legitimate consultants would hold the title of Regulated Canadian Immigration Consultant (RCIC), and that they must uphold a high degree of ethics in order to maintain their license.

A quick search turned up many RCIC's that Aisha could consult. Most surprisingly, they were not actually that much more expensive than the office she had spoken with. In fact, when considering the amount of effort an RCIC would invest in her application, Aisha realized that it would be a much smarter investment to hire an RCIC.

Aisha was also impressed that the RCIC she had selected started the engagement by sharing with her a formal "code of conduct" document that outlined the rights and responsibilities that both she and the RCIC must agree to. She also signed a formal service agreement that outlined clearly the services and fees that had been agreed upon.

The RCIC spent time with Aisha to explain the reasons for her refusal, and was able to recommend some practical steps to take to recover from this situation. They also reviewed all of the paperwork that had been submitted with her first application, and uncovered a lot of mistakes that had been made. Also, the previous consultant did not even write a letter to accompany the application and explain Aisha's situation, her goals, and her ambitions.

A few weeks after a new application was submitted, Aisha was delighted to receive her visa and study permit approval. She was now ready to start planning her trip. But before she did that, she wrote a blog post about her experience, warning others to work with a licensed consultant to avoid the misery that she had faced.

Conclusion

Thinking about studying internationally can be exciting. Being in a new country and meeting people of different backgrounds and cultures, visiting new places, and having new experiences are some of the wonderful rewards of studying abroad. At the same time, being away from family and living in a different country thousands of kilometers away from home can also cause some anxiety. Applying for international universities and worrying about the complexities of applying for a student visa can be overwhelming.

With Canada being a top destination for international students globally, our hope at Ya Hala Canada Immigration is that reading this book has helped to alleviate some of the anxiety and concerns you may have had, especially around getting a study permit. In this book, we discussed some of the advantages of studying in Canada and gave you some background about the country. We also discussed getting admission into a Canadian educational institution, the process for getting a study permit, traveling to Canada, and some of the basic expectations of studying in Canada. We also talked about post-graduation options such as working in Canada or applying for permanent residency.

Many students assume that getting accepted into a university program in Canada automatically means they will receive a student visa and study permit, and that it is just a formality. We hope that after reading this book, you now know the process and the requirements to succeed in your study permit application. Receiving a refusal letter in response to a study permit application can be devastating and can seriously impact your study plans and future. So we hope that the information in this book has helped to prepare you to know what to expect.

However, it is very important to remember that each student's situation is different, and the rules can vary from country to country. Also, the rules and policies change often, and no book could possibly capture all the details and complexities involved. Therefore, this book is to be used as a general guide and overview. Detailed and up-to-date information must be obtained from official sources such as Immigration, Refugees and Citizenship Canada (IRCC). The IRCC has excellent resources, application guides, and step-by-step instructions that are published and updated online[19].

We also highly recommend hiring professional help with any visa or immigration applications to Canada. The cost of such services is well

---

[19] IRCC home page URL:
https://www.canada.ca/en/immigration-refugees-citizenship.html

worth the savings in time, effort, and anxiety that you get by working with a professional. Hire a qualified immigration lawyer or Regulated Canadian Immigration Consultant (RCIC) to make sure you are receiving quality professional services and to avoid being a victim of scams that take advantage of people's desire to immigrate to Canada.

Figure 15: Toronto City Hall [20]

---

[20] **Source:** Maksim Sokolov (maxergon.com), CC BY-SA 4.0 <https://creativecommons.org/licenses/by-sa/4.0>, via Wikimedia Commons
https://commons.wikimedia.org/wiki/File:Toronto_City_Hall_at_Dusk.jpg

Important Legal Notice

- The information provided in this book is:
    - For general information and educational purposes only.
    - It is not to be understood as legal advice or immigration consultation advice.
- Each person's circumstances are unique, and the information in this book may not apply in your situation.
- Program, rules, and regulations change frequently, and some of the information provided in this book may be outdated.
- It is your responsibility to ensure that you are following the processes, rules and regulations for all immigration matters as set by the Government of Canada.
- Ya Hala Canada Immigration Inc. will not be held responsible for any inaccuracies, mistakes, omissions, or outdated information in this document.
- It is highly recommended that you consult with a lawyer or RCIC to discuss your specific circumstances and to ensure that you are following the immigration rules and regulations that apply to your situation at the time of your applications.

About The Author

Raghid Shreih is a Regulated Canadian Immigration Consultant (RCIC). He launched Ya Hala Canada Immigration Inc. in 2018 to help people who are planning to temporarily visit or permanently move to Canada. As an immigrant himself, Raghid knows the challenges and opportunities of immigrating to Canada. He uses this experience, as well as his extensive training and experience in Canadian immigration matters, to advise and guide his clients.

In addition to writing this book to share his knowledge about Canadian study permits, Raghid regularly speaks about immigration matters at events in Canada and globally. Although he is based in Canada, he regularly travels to meet clients in-person around the world, as well as to explore other cultures, societies, and nature.

Raghid has bachelor and master's degrees in Engineering, and a Master's in Business Administration (MBA). You can reach Raghid through his company website: www.yhcvisa.com

Ya Hala Canada Immigration Inc.

Connect With Us For All Your Canada Immigration Needs	
Mailing Address:	73-509 Commissioners Road West London, Ontario, Canada N6J 1Y5
Email:	info@yhcvisa.com
Facebook:	fb.me/yahalacanadaimmigration
Twitter:	@yahalacanada (https://twitter.com/yahalacanada)
Instagram:	https://www.instagram.com/yahala_canada_immigration/
LinkedIn:	https://www.linkedin.com/company/yahala-canada-immigration/

Copyright © 2023 - Ya Hala Canada Immigration Inc. - All rights reserved

Appendix A: Study Permit Approval Rates By Country

Approval rate for Study Permits Applications (excluding Extensions) by IRCC between January 1, 2019 and December 31, 2021 Broken down by year and Country of Residence. [21]

Country of Residence	2019	2020	2021
Grand Total	**60%**	**51%**	**60%**
Afghanistan	8%	8%	10%
Albania	56%	28%	30%
Algeria	23%	15%	19%
Argentina	87%	78%	74%
Armenia	40%	42%	43%
Australia	88%	86%	83%
Austria	84%	99%	95%
Azerbaijan	35%	53%	46%
Bahrain	67%	51%	59%
Bangladesh	42%	37%	46%
Belarus	68%	73%	43%
Belgium	88%	94%	92%

---

[21] Source: https://www.canada.ca/en/immigration-refugees-citizenship/corporate/transparency/committees/cimm-feb-15-17-2022/student-approval-rates.html

Belize	57%	47%	72%
Bermuda	81%	97%	74%
Bolivia	74%	59%	82%
Bosnia-Herzegovina	77%	48%	79%
Brazil	83%	61%	80%
Brunei	70%	43%	88%
Bulgaria	78%	83%	83%
Cambodia	60%	75%	70%
Canada	71%	38%	81%
Chile	82%	91%	91%
Colombia	77%	65%	62%
Costa Rica	64%	61%	76%
Croatia	78%	85%	77%
Cuba	43%	32%	53%
Cyprus	74%	86%	84%
Czech Republic	92%	95%	97%
Denmark	86%	99%	90%
Ecuador	81%	72%	67%
Egypt	54%	52%	55%
El Salvador	61%	28%	64%
Estonia	80%	100%	95%
Ethiopia	13%	22%	14%
Federal Republic of Cameroon	16%	13%	20%
Federal Republic of Germany	90%	98%	96%

Finland	91%	100%	96%
France	93%	98%	92%
Georgia	33%	33%	61%
Ghana	34%	18%	18%
Greece	85%	88%	75%
Guatemala	65%	35%	68%
Honduras	50%	22%	64%
Hong Kong SAR	84%	90%	87%
Hungary	77%	91%	82%
Iceland	67%	59%	53%
India	64%	48%	60%
Iran	44%	46%	39%
Iraq	16%	11%	30%
Italy	92%	97%	95%
Japan	96%	98%	99%
Jordan	35%	23%	23%
Kazakhstan	63%	60%	59%
Kenya	29%	30%	32%
Korea, Republic of	95%	97%	96%
Kuwait	55%	46%	56%
Kyrgyzstan	41%	35%	54%
Lebanon	49%	57%	52%
Lithuania	77%	78%	79%
Luxembourg	97%	100%	94%

Macedonia	36%	55%	78%
Malaysia	86%	81%	74%
Mexico	81%	81%	87%
Morocco	57%	55%	51%
New Zealand	87%	93%	86%
Nicaragua	49%	30%	67%
Nigeria	17%	18%	34%
Norway	88%	96%	85%
Oman	80%	70%	69%
Pakistan	29%	33%	37%
Palestinian Authority (Gaza/West Bank)	23%	25%	16%
Panama, Republic of	81%	74%	87%
Paraguay	61%	83%	85%
People's Republic of China	85%	81%	84%
Peru	74%	67%	78%
Philippines	62%	50%	64%
Poland	83%	97%	90%
Portugal	87%	89%	86%
Qatar	59%	43%	57%
Republic of Indonesia	79%	71%	72%
Republic of Ireland	93%	82%	94%
Republic of Ivory Coast	34%	26%	35%
Republic of South Africa	62%	59%	73%
Romania	75%	51%	77%

Russia	73%	74%	67%
Saudi Arabia	59%	47%	54%
Senegal	25%	19%	26%
Serbia, Republic of	77%	80%	83%
Singapore	85%	94%	92%
Slovak Republic	95%	95%	97%
Slovenia	88%	86%	94%
Socialist Republic of Vietnam	49%	61%	70%
Spain	95%	97%	96%
Sri Lanka	45%	45%	52%
Sweden	84%	96%	93%
Switzerland	87%	98%	90%
Syria	27%	19%	25%
Tadjikistan	16%	33%	38%
Taiwan	92%	93%	88%
Thailand	81%	83%	83%
The Netherlands	91%	95%	93%
Tunisia	59%	64%	50%
Turkey	73%	66%	47%
Turkmenistan	21%	18%	18%
Ukraine	65%	72%	76%
United Arab Emirates	59%	57%	62%
United Republic of Tanzania	59%	44%	55%
United States of America	84%	94%	89%

Uruguay	95%	92%	74%
Uzbekistan	34%	20%	16%
Venezuela	45%	50%	57%
Yemen, Republic of	21%	25%	18%
Zambia	40%	38%	49%
Zimbabwe	24%	26%	49%

Appendix B: CRS Points Grid [22]

(as on November 6, 2022)

Comprehensive Ranking System (CRS) Criteria – Express Entry

Note: If your spouse or partner is not coming with you to Canada, or they are a Canadian citizen or permanent resident, you will earn points as if you don't have a spouse or partner.

Summary of maximum points per factor for Express Entry candidates

A. Core / human capital factors

Factors	With spouse / common-law partner	Without spouse / common-law partner
Age	100	110
Level of education	140	150
Official languages proficiency	150	160
Canadian work experience	70	80

---

[22] Source: https://www.canada.ca/en/immigration-refugees-citizenship/services/immigrate-canada/express-entry/eligibility/criteria-comprehensive-ranking-system/grid.html

B. Spouse or common-law partner factors

Factors	Points per factor (Maximum 40 points)
Level of education	10
Official language proficiency	20
Canadian Work Experience	10

A + B = Maximum 500 points (with OR without a spouse or common-law partner)

C. Skill Transferability factors (Maximum 100 points)

Education	Points per factor (Max 50 points)
With good/strong official languages proficiency **and** a post-secondary degree	50
With Canadian work experience **and** a post-secondary degree	50

Foreign work experience	Points per factor (Max 50 points)
With good/strong official languages proficiency (Canadian Language Benchmark [CLB] level 7 or higher) **and** foreign work experience	50
With Canadian work experience **and** foreign work experience	50

Certificate of qualification (for people in trade occupations)	Points per factor (Max 50 points)
With good/strong official languages proficiency **and** a certificate of qualification	50

A + B + C = Maximum 600 points

D. Additional points (Maximum 600 points)

Factor	Maximum points per factor
Brother or sister living in Canada (citizen or permanent resident)	15
French language skills	50
Post-secondary education in Canada	30
Arranged employment	200
PN nomination	600

Grand Total = A + B + C + D = Maximum 1200 points

Points breakdown, section by section

CRS – A. Core / human capital factors

- With a spouse or common-law partner: Max 460 points total for all factors.
- Without a spouse or common-law partner: Max 500 points total for all factors.

Age	With a spouse / common-law partner (Max 100 points)	Without a spouse or common-law partner (Maximum 110 points)
17 years of age or less	0	0
18 years of age	90	99
19 years of age	95	105
20 to 29 years of age	100	110
30 years of age	95	105
31 years of age	90	99
32 years of age	85	94
33 years of age	80	88
34 years of age	75	83
35 years of age	70	77
36 years of age	65	72
37 years of age	60	66
38 years of age	55	61
39 years of age	50	55
40 years of age	45	50
41 years of age	35	39
42 years of age	25	28
43 years of age	15	17
44 years of age	5	6
45 years of age or more	0	0

Level of Education	With a spouse or common-law partner (Max 140 points)	Without a spouse or common-law partner (Max 150 points)
Less than secondary school	0	0
Secondary diploma	28	30
One-year degree, diploma or certificate from a university, college, trade or technical school	84	90
Two-year program at a university, college, trade or technical school	91	98
Bachelor's degree OR a three or more year program at a university, college, trade or technical school	112	120
Two or more certificates, diplomas, or degrees. One must be for a program of three or more years	119	128
Master's degree, OR professional degree needed to practice in a licensed profession	126	135
Doctoral level degree (Ph.D.)	140	150

Official languages proficiency - first official language

Max points for each ability (reading, writing, speaking and listening):

- 32 with a spouse or common-law partner
- 34 without a spouse or common-law partner

Canadian Language Benchmark (CLB) level per ability	With a spouse or common-law partner (Max 128 points)	Without a spouse or common-law partner (Max 136 points)
Less than CLB 4	0	0
CLB 4 or 5	6	6
CLB 6	8	9
CLB 7	16	17
CLB 8	22	23
CLB 9	29	31
CLB 10 or more	32	34

Official languages proficiency - second official language

Max points for each ability (reading, writing, speaking and listening):

- 6 with a spouse or common-law partner (up to a combined maximum of 22 points)
- 6 without a spouse or common-law partner (up to a combined maximum of 24 points)

Canadian Language Benchmark (CLB) level per ability	With a spouse or common-law partner (Max 22 points)	Without a spouse or common-law partner (Max 24 points)
CLB 4 or less	0	0
CLB 5 or 6	1	1
CLB 7 or 8	3	3
CLB 9 or more	6	6

Canadian work experience	With a spouse or common-law partner (Max 70 points)	Without a spouse or common-law partner (Max 80 points)
Less than a year	0	0
1 year	35	40
2 years	46	53
3 years	56	64
4 years	63	72
5 years or more	70	80

Subtotal: A. Core / human capital factors

- With a spouse or common-law partner – Max 460 points
- Without a spouse or common-law partner – Max 500 points

CRS – B. Spouse or common-law partner factors (if applicable)

Spouse's or common-law partner's level of education	With spouse or common-law partner (Max 10 points)
Less than secondary school (high school)	0
Secondary school (high school graduation)	2
One-year program at a university, college, trade or technical school	6
Two-year program at a university, college, trade or technical in school	7
Bachelor's degree OR a three or more year program at a university, college, trade or technical school	8
Two or more certificates, diplomas, or degrees. One must be for a program of three or more years	9
Master's degree, or professional degree needed to practice in a licensed profession	10
Doctoral level university degree (PhD)	10

Spouse's or common-law partner's official languages proficiency - first official language

Canadian Language Benchmark (CLB) level per ability (reading, writing, speaking and listening)	Max 20 points (Max 5 points per ability)
CLB 4 or less	0
CLB 5 or 6	1
CLB 7 or 8	3
CLB 9 or more	5

Spouse's Canadian work experience	Maximum 10 points
None or less than a year	0
1 year	5
2 years	7
3 years	8
4 years	9
5 years or more	10

A + B = Maximum 500 points

CRS – C. Skill transferability factors (Maximum 100 points for this section)

Education

With good official language proficiency (Canadian Language Benchmark Level [CLB] 7 or higher) and a post-secondary degree	Points for CLB 7 or more on all first official language abilities, with one or more under CLB 9 (Max 25 points)	Points for CLB 9 or more on all four first official language abilities (Max 50 points)
Secondary school credential or less	0	0
Post-secondary program credential of one year or longer	13	25
Two or more post-secondary program credentials AND at least one of these credentials was issued on completion of a post-secondary program of three years or longer	25	50
A university-level credential at the master's level or at the level of an entry-to-practice professional degree	25	50
A university-level credential at the doctoral level	25	50

With Canadian work experience and a post-secondary degree	Points for education + 1 year of Canadian work experience (Max 25 points)	Points for education + 2 years or more of Canadian work experience (Max 50 points)
Secondary school credential or less	0	0
Post-secondary program credential of one year or longer	13	25
Two or more post-secondary program credentials AND at least one of these credentials was issued on completion of a post-secondary program of three years or longer	25	50
A university-level credential at the master's level or at the level of an entry-to-practice professional degree	25	50
A university-level credential at the doctoral level	25	50

Foreign work experience – With CLB 7 or higher

Years of foreign work experience	Foreign work experience + CLB 7 or more (Max 25 points)	Foreign work experience + CLB 9 or more (Max 50 points)
None	0	0
1 or 2	13	25
3 or more	25	50

Copyright © 2023 - Ya Hala Canada Immigration Inc. - All rights reserved

Foreign work experience – With Canadian work experience

Years of foreign work experience	Foreign work experience + 1 year of Canadian work experience (Max 25 points)	Foreign work experience + 2 years or more of Canadian work experience (Max 50 points)
None	0	0
1 or 2	13	25
3 or more	25	50

Certificate of qualification (trade occupations) – With language proficiency (CLB 5 or higher)	Certificate of qualification + CLB 5 or more (Max 25 points)	Certificate of qualification + CLB 7 or more (Max 50 points)
With a certificate of qualification	25	50

A + B + C = Maximum 600 points

CRS – D. Additional points (Maximum 600 points)

Additional points	Maximum 600 points
Brother or sister living in Canada who is a citizen or permanent resident of Canada	15
Scored NCLC 7 or higher on all four French language skills and scored CLB 4 or lower in English (or didn't take an English test)	25
Scored NCLC 7 or higher on all four French language skills and scored CLB 5 or higher on all four English skills	50
Post-secondary education in Canada - credential of one or two years	15
Post-secondary education in Canada - credential three years or longer	30
Arranged employment - NOC 00	200
Arranged employment – any other NOC 0, A or B	50
Provincial or territorial nomination	600

Grand Total = A + B + C + D = Maximum 1200 points

www.ingramcontent.com/pod-product-compliance
Lightning Source LLC
Chambersburg PA
CBHW051539020426
42333CB00016B/1998